"If you know  .y and know yourself, you need not fear the result of a hundred battles. If you know yourself but not the enemy, for every victory gained you will also suffer a defeat. If you know neither the enemy nor yourself, you will succumb in every battle."

      - Sun Tzu, The Art of War

"A guy came up to me at the gym and asked me what event I was training so hard for. Life, motherfucker."

      - Overheard on the @GSElevator

Foreword:

The goal of this book is to help you get a job in investment banking. The intended audience of this book is undergraduates, MBAs or anyone looking to make an early in career change. It is based on hundreds of interviews that I have received as a candidate, given as a investment bank hiring manager or heard about first hand.

For the past five years, I've been writing this book in front of a live audience, in the form of advice I give at the end of finance seminars. I've taught thousands of students who say my advice is valuable and unlike any they've ever received. In response to many requests for my notes, I've written this book.

I want you to get inside the head of the hiring manager to better understand what he or she is looking for in a candidate. To understand your adversary (and it is an adversarial process) is to be prepared. Some of the thoughts and language used in this book may seem a bit matter of fact, to the point and even a bit callous. If you find yourself not wanting to work for or with such a person, you might want to consider other career paths. It doesn't get better.

In writing this book, I'm attempting to make a serious subject somewhat entertaining. In doing so, it may appear the bad and the ugly sometimes rise over the good. I wouldn't be writing this book if I didn't think investment banking was the greatest of careers. Speaking of ugly, any resemblance to real people, living or dead, is entirely coincidental.

I've helped place dozens of people at such top investment banks as Goldman Sachs, Bank of America, Barclays, Citibank, etc. (as well as many other financial and consulting firms). I found great joy in helping people break into the club. And it is a club. The good news is that once you are in, you are in. The skills conveyed in this book are intended to help you break into the club. I have no doubt this book will help you too break into investment banking. Be careful what you wish for.

Table of Contents

Section 1: Getting the Interview
- The hiring manager
- No story no offer
- Know your audience

Section 2: Preparing for the Interview
- A serious game
- Super day

Section 3: Acing the Interview
- Types of questions
- To do's and not to do's

Section 4: Post Interview
- Careful what you wish for
- You got the job
- You didn't get the job
- Closing
- Q&A

Section 1: Getting the Interview

Chapter 1: The Hiring Manager

It's late at night and I want to go home. The person from HR has been pestering me for a week to get her my candidates for Super Day. "Fuck you I work for a living," I think, not totally oblivious, just indifferent, to anyone's plight but my own.

I had my assistant print out over 200 resumes and cover letters (bankers kill a lot of trees), which are sitting on my desk in a neat stack and have been eyeing me for days. It's now 10pm; I've been at the office all day and again I want to go home. We're hiring two associates and three analysts for this summer's class. Per HR, I need to pick about ten candidates by close of business today. "Well you didn't say whose close of business," I think (along with a few more obscenities) as I reach for the stack of papers.

What I'm about to say may sound cruel and heartless. I offer no apologies. I want you to get inside the head of whom you are dealing with. I pick the first cover letter and resume (neatly stapled) off of the stack. Your cover page and your resume should be two pages (one each). If you have more than two pages (which I can feel from the weight in my hand), I assume you think you are more important than you should and I'm more inclined to ding you. By ding, I mean toss your papers in the trash. Fair to you? Probably not, but it's late and I want to go home, and more than two pages is wasting my time.

I quickly scan the cover letter. Here's what I'm looking for:
- Does it look professional, meaning does it look like a college or business school student wrote it and not your third grade sister?
- Is it free of typos?
- Did you remember to cut and paste (or find and replace) the name of the other banks from which you repurposed the template. Don't think I don't know you do that.
- Is it short and sweet and to the point?
- Can you form a logical argument and structure (topic paragraph, supporting thoughts, closing paragraph)?

If your cover letter answers "yes" to all of the above, I flip the page. If there are any "no's" to above, I may or may not flip the page to look at your resume, largely depending on: 1) where you are in the stack (and how many candidates I have left to go), and 2) my general curiosity (also influenced by how many candidates I have left to go). This process took me about 15 seconds. Note that I skimmed but did not read your cover letter. Again, it's late and I want to go home.

Let's assume I do flip the page to your resume. Here's what I'm looking for:
- Does it look professional?
- Do you go to a good school and have a good GPA?
- Does your most recent work experience say finance?
- Do I think you are interesting based on your skills and interests?

If your resume answers "yes" to all of the above (and you passed the cover letter test), I put you in the YES pile. If your resume answered "no" to more than one of these questions, I put you in the NO pile. If your resume answered "no" to one of those questions (e.g. low GPA), but you were very strong in another (e.g. you play a sport), then I'm most likely going to put you in the MAYBE pile. This whole process takes me about 30 to 45 seconds. Fair to you? No way. I know you are worth more than a minute of my time, but again, it's late and I want to go home. You are standing in my way.

When I hit the bottom of the original pile of 200, I pick up the NO pile and throw it in the trash. Sorry, better luck next time. Next I pick up the YES pile and see how many made the cut. If it's more than about 15 (I need a few backup candidates), I start the process over now with a little more rigor. Again, same questions but now I'm just grading harder. If the YES pile is less than 15, I turn to the MAYBE pile and do the same. If I find my 15 then I take the MAYBE pile and throw it out (perhaps salvaging one or two that I wanted as additional backup). I then take my list of 15 names and reply back to the HR manager with a simple "These are the people I want to bring in, rank ordered." It's midnight and I finally get to go home.

Chapter 2: No Story No Offer

Four little words are all you need to remember. It's as simple as that. If you don't have a story for why you want to be an i-banker, you are not going to get the job. There is no work around. There is no getting lucky. There is no creating it on the fly. If you don't have a good story you will not get an offer. Period.

So what's a story then? Simply put, it's everything you've done to date that has prepared you to become an i-banker. Sounds simple right? Softball right? I mean after all, who can tell me more about you than you? Guess again.

You will often get questions like, "Tell me about yourself", or "Walk me through your resume", or "Why do you want to do i-banking", or the always popular "What brings you in today?" The goal of these questions is to get to your story. And remember your story is: 1) everything you've done to date, 2) that has prepared you for i-banking. Note that the second part of that last sentence is key. It's not everything you've done. This is where people often make the first mistake. You start with something like, "Well I was born in...." I don't care where you were born. Or you may start with, "I grew up in...." Again, I don't care where you grew up. Or perhaps you go back to high school. Sorry, but likely irrelevant. None of these answers address the second part of your story, namely "that has prepared you for i-banking". If you're talking about something that doesn't address part 2 of your story, I'm thinking about work you are making me miss. No job for you.

Your story should be short and to the point. I want to hear your story in 45 to 60 seconds max. If you are still talking after two minutes, my eyes may be looking at you but I assure you I'm no longer listening. What my brain is thinking is, this person doesn't have a good story, so I'm not going to give them an offer. Actually, I'm more likely thinking, "Will you shut the fuck up already?" Is that fair to you? No. If we were anywhere else, I'm sure I'd love to hear about all of your great experiences, but not here, not now. If I don't hear your story told the way I want to hear it, you will not be able to recover. That softball is a swing and miss and there is no next pitch.

So what is your story? Well unfortunately only you can craft your story. I think I can help, but ultimately your story will differ from everyone else because your experiences are unique (although it may not feel like it). Your story takes practice. Your story requires you to stand in front of the mirror and deliver it out loud. Your story requires you trying it with your friends and classmates. Your story evolves. Your story is a living breathing narrative of your experiences and why they have prepared you for a career in i-banking.

For some people their story is easy. Recently I worked with someone in a one on one setting who wanted to work at Goldman Sachs. When I asked him what his story was, he said, "I am a rising senior studying economics at (Ivy League school). I am the president of the finance club and help oversee our multi-million dollar investment fund. My father and two older brothers work at Goldman Sachs. Since childhood, I've prepared myself to work at Goldman." Well guess where he works? You guessed it.

But everyone's story is not that simple. Let me tell you about my story coming out of business school. I remember one interview very well. It was two (of them) on one (of me) in about a 4-foot by 4-foot room. Fair? Not really, but we'll get to that later. I think the bank was JP Morgan. Interviewer one sees my resume and says, "So why do you want to be a banker?" My response started with, "Well I went back to business school because I wanted to work in finance." She frowned a bit at my response and actually stopped me and said, "I didn't ask why you went back to business school, but rather why you want to be a banker." So I started again, "Well, you see, I was working for America Online in their nascent Internet advertising group and I found I really enjoyed working with numbers but realized I needed to go back to business school to refine my skills." I think at this point she kind of turned her head sideways (like a dog does) and interrupted me again with, "But why i-banking?" At this point I was becoming a bit frustrated. I honestly thought I was answering the question. I absolutely went back to business school because I wanted to work in finance. But I wasn't answering her question. The rest of the interview went well but guess what? No job for me. My story failed. Despite multiple attempts, I still bombed and I didn't even realize why.

During another interview in business school, the woman sitting across from me welcomed me, asked me to take a seat, picked up my resume and said, "Why did you go to Virginia Tech?" That's an easy warm up question out of the gate right? I answered with something like, "Well where I'm from 90% of my high-school goes to Virginia Tech." To which she replied, "Do you do everything your friends do?" Guess what? No job for me. The rest of the interview didn't matter. One 30 second question that was about my story, and I failed.

Compare and contrast that to my business school classmates who were former bankers but went back to business school because they wanted to change careers. Every one of them got multiple investment banking offers. Why? Because their story was already clear. They were already in the club so the fact that they wanted to do something else wasn't part of their story, at least in the interviews. So they took the sure thing. And those that actually wanted to do investment banking had to fight for the scraps. See what you're up against? I hope you also see the potential.

You may have heard the expression "the elevator test". It's usually reserved for entrepreneurs trying to pitch their business idea to a venture capitalist. For example, rather than explaining the value of a mobile logistics platform that matches customers with operators of private jets, you could simply say, "It's like Uber for private jets." Which story is clearer?

In this case, the elevator test also applies to you. If you are riding with a hiring manager in the elevator from their office on the 30th floor down to the lobby and you have 45 seconds to convince them you are the right person for the job, that's your story. This is the most important and perhaps the most challenging part of the interview.

As you think about your story, ask yourself some questions:
- Is there anything prior to college (if you're in college) or prior to graduate school (if you're in business school) that is relevant to your story?
- What have you done in school, an internship or in your personal life that is finance related?
- How have you shown progression in your experiences that have positioned you for the job (and firm) for which you are currently interviewing?
- Are there other leadership or team experiences that can relate to the i-banking culture?

You don't have to have a perfect story. Few do. Let me repeat, you don't need to be an Ivy League educated son of a Goldman Sachs senior banker who carries a 4.0 in your finance related major. It's often not that clean.

You can work with a mediocre story, so long as it is a story. I've known many a banker whose parents didn't know what i-banking was, who had less than a 3.5 GPA (the bank advertised cut off point), and who majored in English or History. I once hired a candidate with a 3.0 GPA who majored in Latin. Who even studies Latin anymore? But she had a great story of why she wanted to be a banker. I also once knew an amazing banker who was a theater major and actually worked on Broadway for four years before going back to B-school and becoming a first-rate banker. Think about that story for a second (never mind what it says about an i-banking career).

Your story may take a bit of time to craft but don't shortchange yourself. Those 45 seconds will make or break you. Practice it with your classmates. Practice it in the shower. Practice it while you're exercising. Practice it as you are falling asleep. It will evolve in your head. Keep practicing until you get to a point where it feels good to you. Then practice it again. If you do nothing else, put down this book and practice your story for a few hours.

As for my story, it took many years to develop. I was a pre-med major in college who took a business class my senior year and fell in love. I went on to work for an internet company in their online advertising group where I worked with numbers all day and I was even more in love. After a major merger at the aforementioned AOL (which has gone down as the worst merger in history), I decided to go back to school to pursue my business education. From there I chose consulting out of the gate and helped companies do business better. That led to helping large corporations start new digital companies. I decided I wanted to follow my passion and grow my skills at a technology focused investment bank. So I did. My story took about 30 seconds but it was a more than four-year evolution.

Chapter 3: Know Your Audience

A common question you will get in an investment banking interview is, "Tell me what I do." What a horrible question to ask you. How dare they ask you that? You've never done their job. But you want to, so it is a fair game question. In fact, it's a great question to see if you have done your research. More on that research you should do later, but let's learn a little more about your interviewers.

Generally speaking, bankers are Type A, which means we like to be in control, we like to win or at least be right and we don't (like to) make mistakes. We are also the most detail oriented people you will ever meet. I recall a former MD (stands for managing director, not medical doctor, though they often believe they are just as important) who could spot a mistake in my work in ten seconds flat. I used to call it the ten-second test. I would work on a spreadsheet for hours and he could spot calculation errors and font mistakes in seconds. (Note: there is an unwritten rule of i-banking that the more you stare at your computer screen the less you see your mistakes. A fresh set of eyes always brings a new perspective. Have someone read your resume and cover letter for typos and inconsistencies. If they don't find it, I probably will.)

At the same time, we live in an interruption driven world, so the ability to jump from task to task is a desired banker skill. In some bankers, this is full on Attention Deficit Disorder (ADD). (Note: I had someone once tell me they were offended I described ADD, which they had, as a skill. First, I meant it partly as a joke but also to highlight that it is common. Second, to that person with the disability, if you think I get enjoyment making fun of people with disabilities, go fuck yourself, and by the way, this is the wrong career for you.)

So let's talk about the people you will meet. We'll start with one of my previous firms. I remember it well. I got an email the day before I was starting letting me know to bring a change of clothes the first day because we had front row seats to the Yankees Red Sox season opener. Turns out the firm had season tickets, which I would come to enjoy as one of the better perks of the job. I also recall my MD (we'll call him James) telling me in tears many years later that his soon to be ex-wife had requested an itemized list of every person that ever attended a game and all associated expenses. Ouch. I too was going through a divorce at the time. Bankers often bond over misery.

I recall that first day well. It would be the earliest I'd ever leave work (7:10pm game). My desk was in a small room with another associate while the analysts shared a slightly larger "bullpen". I felt like a lion in a cage, especially when others came by to talk to me. That was rare unless they needed something. Mostly people showed up to work, went to their office and closed their doors. Not a warm and fuzzy place. On that first day, one of the MDs (we'll call him Roger) came by and said, "Feel free to take off your (suit) jackets while in the office, but make sure you put them back on if you leave." That included going to the bathroom which was down the hall. Roger would later become a little softer and once said, "Feel free to get your hair cut on company time, because after all it grows on company time."

What I remember most from that first day is all the code names people used. Bankers don't want names of companies getting out in the public (for good reason, it's called jail), so they speak in code. One banker may not even know the company his counterpart is working on, simply the codename. The fewer names, the less risk of insider trading. I recall being put on my first deal that day. It was a divestiture of a major technology company's subsidiary to an Irish private equity (PE) shop. On a conference call when asked about the status of a group of people's jobs post-merger, someone actually said, "That's below my pay grade." Now I recall hearing, "That's above my pay grade," but this person was actually saying they were too important to worry about it. "Welcome to the big leagues," I thought. On that call there was also concern over the subsidiary's working capital going forward. (Note: you will often get the technical question of, "What is working capital and why is it important?") Essentially the subsidiary had negative working capital and the PE shop was threatening to walk or cut the deal value. They had been at an impasse for a few days. I remember when the call ended (unsuccessfully) that I piped up and said, "Why don't we just wipe the balance sheet, it's influenced by the parent company anyway?" The MD looked at me but didn't say anything. Two days later that's exactly what happened. I'm not saying I saved the deal, but sometimes it helps to have a new perspective. I also recall ordering my business cards that day, with lots of *American Psycho* quotes flying. (Note: You'll be tempted to ask a banker who hands you their cards if it is "egg shell with Roman" or "raised lettering pale nimbus" but don't.

They will get the joke but you won't get the job. And yes my card did have a watermark.)

Let's talk about some of the people I worked with daily. The following names and likenesses have been changed to protect the innocent (and guilty). At my firm there were four personas best qualified in my direct team. These are the people who will interview you so get to know them now.

- James the "sales guy": James was a Managing Director. He was an Ivy League educated, history major who came from a family of bankers. He was American but somehow went to British military boarding school (picture the opposite physique of James Bond, with a serious sweating problem). He started his career as a trader (at his dad's bank, which he owned) but on his merit rose to head of investment banking at a major bulge bracket bank. He had more tombstones than anyone I've ever met. A tombstone is a glass (Lucite actually) reminder of a completed deal, naming the parties and deal value. You can often gauge a banker's ego by the number of tombstones he or she has on the bookshelf. Strangely, it's often an inverse relationship. He lived in the nicest neighborhood in town and sat on the boards of several public committees. He fancied himself a serious musician, but it was more accurately a hobby masked by a lot of money thrown at it. He had ADD to the 9th degree. I recall once watching him open nine Amazon packages while on a very important conference call (which he didn't bother to mute) where the buyer was threatening to walk. (In retrospect, what a great strategy!) He carried three phones. I once watched him manage three calls on those three phones while smoking a cigarette outside of a technology conference. He was an amazing sales person, who got people (employees and clients) to do things they didn't want to do. He had an amazing ability to motivate as well as highlight the positives in any situation. There was a time I would have named my son after him. It took me, and many others, time to learn he was evil at heart. He eventually betrayed and alienated everyone around him. Be prepared to interview with the "sales guy".

- Roger "the analytical mind": Roger was also a Managing Director. Another Ivy League educated history major, but he was twenty years younger than James. What he lacked in tombstones he made up for in previous job titles, which included rising through the i-banking ranks right out of undergrad, to Ivy League MBA, to manager of a bank's international office, to MD, to venture capitalist then back to MD. He is, to this day, one of the smartest people I've ever met. He taught me more about modeling than almost anyone, and his attention to detail was second to none. He used to ask me, "Adam, did you check this with a calculator?" My answer was always, "Well no Roger, because I used Excel and it's the world's most powerful calculator." To which he'd reply, "Well you should learn how to use it because you made a mistake." He'd throw the paper back at me. It didn't hurt, it was just paper after all, but my pride hurt as I walked back to my desk to check. "No fucking way I made a mistake," I thought, but he was always right. (Note: always bring a calculator to an i-banking interview. You will probably need it and you don't want to look unprepared. More importantly, you want to be perceived like the person sitting across from you, and I guarantee you they have a calculator with them.) Roger was also the most honest banker I ever met. He could not and would not tell a lie. I respected that the most. Be prepared to interview with the "analytical mind".

- Bob "the apprehensive": Bob and I worked on many deals together. He was a VP and thus a level above me, and he was always worried about something. He'd worry we wouldn't find a buyer for a company we were selling (by the way, that's called a sell-side deal; when you are representing the buyer of another company it's called a buy side deal). When we found a buyer, he'd worry they wouldn't pay what the seller wanted. When they agreed to the price, he'd worry they would walk. You get the gist. And I'm not talking normal level of worry, I'm talking Mylanta for breakfast, Vodka for dinner, the world is going to end kind of worry. I'm sure it didn't help that Bob was a lawyer in a previous life. In actuality, I learned more about M&A from Bob through his legal lens than anyone. He became a brother in arms, the kind of person you want next to you in a foxhole when there is a battle (no disrespect to the veterans that may be reading this, but I know you know what I mean). Be prepared to interview with "the apprehensive".

- George "the busy body": George was a Director at the bank but more importantly an Ivy League classmate and friend of James. He boasted of his east coast boarding school upbringing and every new client he brought into the firm was usually a classmate from said boarding school. Although he rarely dropped his last name in business, it was a name that you would likely recognize from the Gilded Age. A colleague once described George as the embodiment of "WASP rot". At one time his family was one of the richest in America, but it didn't show by the Prius he drove. When I worked with him he was so proud to argue why he was paying off his mortgage as interest rates dropped. I guess intelligence is not a prerequisite to inheriting family money. George was always flying to France, England or some other country to do "business development" which is short for meeting with some industry magnate who was going to do a big deal. In the many years I worked with him, he never closed a single deal, yet he was always busy and quick to let everyone know how important he was. I found such enjoyment once during our Monday morning team call (where everyone provided an update on the deals they were working on) pointing out that a client (and a childhood boarding school friend) he was supposedly representing had just closed a deal of which he wasn't aware. The MDs grilled him on the details of the target, which of course he didn't know. They then grilled him on the status of our engagement, which he had just represented as "on track". The MDs literally told him to leave the meeting and I did my best to suppress a smile. There is nothing worse in my opinion than someone who thinks they are more important than they are. Near the start of the financial crisis, George was the one who told me I would have to take a part-time role the day after I closed the bank's largest deal ever. James didn't have the stones. Last I heard George was trying his hand at farming. While the thought of him up to his ankles in cow shit brings me some joy, I suppose it's harder to do nothing on a farm. Be prepared to interview with the "self-important busy body".

Of course there were others but they fit the above molds. There was the very successful equity research analyst (during the tech bubble) turned unsuccessful movie producer (who invested millions of her own money), turned unsuccessful M&A banker. Busy body. There was the Dutch Excel wiz who everyone picked on, but he could out calculate anyone, except maybe Roger. Analytical mind. There was the adult Harry Potter look alike who closed more deals than anyone but never said anything to anyone unless asked. Sales guy in an analytical mind disguise. There was the attractive future caretaker to the children of an NBA team owner (speaking of bad M&A deals), turned management consultant. Analytical mind.

I want you to picture the culture you will be working in and the people you will be working with as an investment banker. Sound fun? Sound like a place you'd like to work? Sound like people you'd like to spend 12 hours a day with? You bet! Again, I wouldn't be writing this book if I didn't think it was the greatest job in the world but I want you to know what to expect to better prepare yourself.

Section 2: Preparing for the Interview

Chapter 4: A Serious Game

I want you to think about preparing for the interview like you would prepare for a game, any game. Before you take to the field, board, screen or other location, you've likely put in hours of practice. Now think of your favorite athlete. How much time do you think they spend preparing? It is said that some of the best athletes can visualize components of the game or match prior to the actual event. Whether it is a batter envisioning a home run or a golfer seeing a perfect tee shot, the principle is the same; their minds know what to expect before it happens.

Apply that same principle to your i-banking interviews. Visualize the setting: a small conference room with an external window highlighting another skyscraper next door and an internal window with lots of people outside looking up from their multiple computer screens. You're not quite sure what to think. Are they looking at you as potential competition, or as a lamb about to be led to slaughter? Truth be told, it's probably a bit of both. There's a large and expensive TV on the wall and you wonder which business leaders have sat in your seat. You wonder what types of deals have been reviewed on the screen. The conference table is a polished expensive wood and the chairs are more comfortable than they should be. There is a formality to it, mixed with an air of opulence and fear of the unknown.

Now visualize the other interviewees in the conference room. All are nicely dressed, carrying leather folders in hope of protection, like a shield their parents gave them as they branch out in the world. One or two act like they already belong. Others look confident that they have gotten this far. Most look afraid and are wearing it better than their suit.

Now visualize your interviewer. He or she comes to collect you from the conference room. Your gut reaction is this is a nicely dressed person with bad coffee breath who isn't smiling a lot. You follow them along the side of the large open office. More eyes watch you. Some smile, some smirk and some don't make eye contact.

He or she points you into an office and you enter. It's small, with one desk and two computer screens. "Take a seat," he says, and you do. He shuts the door and picks up your resume. Sometimes it's two or three of them against one of you.

I hope you get the picture. It will evolve the more interviews you attend but the basics will stay with you. What are you thinking right now? You're probably thinking, "I hope you don't ask me anything too technical." Or maybe you're thinking, "Does this person likes me? Have I made a good first impression?" Or perhaps you are thinking, "I can't believe I have three more of these today."

What you should be thinking is, "I'm ready for this." Or maybe, "There is no place I'd rather be right now." Or something like, "Give me all you got because I see myself getting this job and this is just the next step in the process."

You are prepared for what is about to happen. The nicely dressed person(s) sitting across from you is about to make your life difficult. That person(s) will enjoy making you squirm a little (or a lot). Why? Well there are two theories. The first being that someone did it to them so they learned the behavior. The second is they are sadistic sons (and daughters) of bitches and they enjoy inflicting pain. While either (or both of those) might be true, actually they are just trying to weed out those who don't belong. And that's a good thing for them and for you.

Understand that a banker has unconscious bias and use it to your advantage. By unconscious bias I mean:

- Stereotype – unfortunately things like age, race and gender will be one's first unconscious bias towards you; there's nothing you can do other than be proud of the person you are. Whatever you are, use it to your advantage. If you played sports, let me know that I'm sitting across from the next Tom Brady in the boardroom. If you're older than the other candidates, let me know how much more experienced and sure of yourself you are. Whoever you are, be you.

- First impressions – make a great first impression because it's the only one you get. I know we were told to not judge a book by its cover, but unfortunately many people do. So make sure you shine in those first few moments.

- Like me – if you are perceived like them, then you are more likely to get hired. Whether we acknowledge it or not, we're more inclined to hire people like us, so make sure you are like that person sitting across from you. This includes speaking their financial language, dressing like them, carrying a calculator like them, sitting like them, etc.

- Halo / non-halo effect – if the interviewer is impressed then other things will appear more positive; vice versa for the non-halo. This usually takes the perception of an interview going well or not going well, but be careful to not blow it as the halo can quickly come off if you screw up. Unfortunately it's hard to find the halo once it's gone.

- Self-fulfilling – once the interviewer has an image of you, they look for evidence to support their conclusion. That conclusion can be good or bad depending on the above. Again, just acknowledge people act this way and try to give them the best image possible.

So, I said treat it like a game, but that doesn't mean it's not serious. It is. I can assure you the person(s) sitting across from you will treat it like a game, and the objective is to see if you have what it takes to do their job (or at first help them do their job). What is more important than finding someone who can help them, who knows what the job is all about, who is going to be there all night and weekends, who isn't going to flame out after a few months, who is going to absorb the stresses of the job and ask for more, who is going to grow in responsibility, who will one day be working side by side with the interviewer in front of an unhappy client, and who is going to do the same thing as he/she is doing right now by picking that same person again? There is nothing more important than that, except for maybe one thing, which is whether or not they like you, but more on that later.

As for you, you too need to treat it like a game of equal significance. After all, what is more important than finding a job you like, with people you like (or can at least tolerate), which is going to keep you challenged, where there is opportunity to grow, and you see yourself working for many years. There is nothing more important than that.

If you go in expecting the interview to be smooth, then when it does start to get challenging, and it will, you will not be prepared. What this usually looks like to the interviewer is a deer in the headlights. Eyes wide. Frozen. Not breathing. It's not a good visual, but that is what the interviewer sees. They see fear. They see uncertainty. And they are going to run you over like a Mack truck doing 65 mph. Why? Simple. They don't want someone who is afraid to do their job. Fear means weakness and weakness means you are likely to leave them in a lurch. They want to prove to themselves you don't have what it takes, so they will (see self-fulfilling bias above). No job for you.

It's very important that you be confident but not cocky. Sometimes people overcompensate for their nervousness by acting cocky, like they know it all (or like they were born with a Goldman Sachs birthmark on their ass). While that may be true, cockiness is a recipe for disaster. If I see someone acting cocky, I'm going to make sure they're not any more by the time they leave. Only one of us will enjoy that process.

I mentioned one other very important thing the interviewer is looking for, that is, do they like you? I'm not saying they want to leave the interview and go grab a beer, go shopping, or do whatever you're in to, but have you somehow created a bond with that person? This is commonly referred to as the airport test. Would I mind being stuck in an airport with you (a frequent occurrence) or am I at the bar drinking my sorrows away? I'm reminded of a cold Boston winter during which Bob and I were in Dallas, TX, working on a deal. We arrived at the airport to find our flight two hours delayed (fucking airlines), so we sat outside and sunned ourselves for those two hours. That's called passing the airport test.

Chapter 5: Super Day

So you got the interview? You've been invited, along with five to ten other promising individuals, to spend a Saturday with your new prospective colleagues. Why a Saturday? Well, because they are at the office anyway and you should get used to it too. The day will be exciting and exhausting. You will be completely bored and utterly challenged. You will feel important yet insignificant. Welcome to investment banking.

What now? First make sure you know where you are going. There's nothing worse than showing up late for an interview (ok, maybe wearing a tuxedo...*Step Brothers* reference). If you need to, walk from your hotel to the office the night before and determine how long you will need (add time based on rush hour traffic).

Next, be prepared to wait in a conference room. And wait. And wait. And wait. Allow yourself about twice as much time as they said you would need to be there. If they said three hours, plan on six. If they said four hours, plan on eight. Any more than that and you should plan to be there the whole day (meaning don't schedule your return trip until the next day).

Why are they making you wait? Well firstly, they are busy running live deals with demanding clients which take priority. Once things get backed up, it usually has an amplifying effect the rest of the day (often this results in multiple interviewers on one interviewee situations to make up for lost time). Settle in and try to get comfortable as you wait. What shouldn't happen is you telling anyone you need to leave in an hour to catch your flight. All they hear is you don't want to work there. No job for you.

So you're in the conference room waiting for someone to call you into their office. You need to look busy. You need to look studious. You need to look like you are a hard worker. You are being watched. Not in the security camera, let's throw a baby lamb in and see what they do now kind of way, but every time someone comes in, or even walks by the conference room, they are looking to see what you are doing. Perception is reality. If you're staring at the ceiling, you're a slacker. If you're texting on your phone, you're easily distracted. If you're playing Angry Birds, making the body movements with each strategic shot, they may ask you to leave. You want to be perceived as a hard worker. This involves bringing a (non-fiction) book, a (financial) magazine or newspaper, or some homework. I realize this isn't fair and they are wasting your time, but don't blow it before you even get a chance to open your mouth.

Be cordial with the other interviewees. They may be your colleagues one day. You can exchange pleasantries, but that's it. Don't talk sports. Don't talk school. Don't talk pop culture. Don't friend each other on Facebook and compare people you know in common. No checking Tinder. Don't talk about what's happening in each interview. Don't laugh and have a grand old time. If you do, then they see a troublemaker. No job for you.

While you are in the conference room, if you have the opportunity for a leadership moment, take it. What do I mean by leadership moment? Well let's say Banker Jane walks in and calls out Interviewee Tim's name. You know that Tim is in with Banker Joe and hasn't returned yet, so you speak up. Now you've jumped off the page to Jane. That's a leadership moment. Now I'm not saying you need to take roll or ask people where they are going and when they will be back. Don't worry, you will have plenty of time to be anal once in the job. You're tracking with what's going on and that's more than most people. If the interviewer asks whom you've spoken with already, know their names and a few topic sentences summarizing what you've talked about. If you're searching in your folder for their business cards, they see someone who can't remember details. If someone comes in and says they will be ordering food for the group, take the role of collecting the orders. Leadership moment.

While you are waiting, try to keep your energy up. I don't know about you, but when I haven't eaten for a while I get cranky, and that shouldn't be you. So, if you need to bring some food to the interview, do it, just make sure it's not going to stink up the place or make a mess.

Now they call you in to their office. Finally. When they do, you are excited to be there. You are happy that they've made you wait. You are ecstatic that they've wasted your time. As far as they are concerned, there is nowhere else you'd rather be and nothing you'd rather be doing. If you show any displeasure in having had to wait, no job for you.

If you sense any frustration or consternation in your interviewer, be cautious. Bankers are generally negative by nature (or at least after a few years on the job). It may come off like, "Sorry I'm late, I had a difficult client situation I was trying to resolve." Or if they are really having a bad day perhaps they may say, "Hey, sorry we're backed up, there never seems to be enough hours in the day." Do not feed into this negativity. It is a trap. If you say, "Yeah I hear you about the tough clients," or "Yeah, I know the feeling," then they will quickly look at you like "What the fuck do you know?" And guess what? No job for you. Answer with a simple, "Of course, not a problem." You'll have plenty of time to be negative once you're in the job, but right now you want the tough clients and you want the tough days. There is nothing you'd rather do. Stay away from the negativity traps.

As you get called into the office, be prepared to get grilled, filleted, skewered, or any other cooking reference you'd like (deep fried is a possibility). In the next chapter, we'll talk at length about the types of questions you will be asked. First, let's talk about the interview setting. Be prepared to be in the hot seat. By that I mean, they are about to turn up the heat literally and figuratively. You very well might be sitting in an actual hot seat assuming they have a window and the sun is beating down on you in a full suit as you begin to sweat a little and then a lot.

There will be one to three of them versus one of you. In the one on one situation, you should be prepared to have a conversation with that person. That includes keeping both feet on the ground. Make eye contact. Don't cross your arms. If they ask you if you want some water, take them up on the offer (James the "sales guy" once taught me that trick; if they didn't want to get you water they wouldn't have asked, and if you say no you put them on the defensive).

In the two on one scenario, you will often get a "good cop bad cop" situation. Take it in stride. You're not likely going to turn the "bad cop" so don't try. And the "good cop" can just as easily give you a thumbs down while the "bad cop" may like you.

It gets a little more challenging if it's three on one. In the worst-case scenario, one person will be grilling you. Another person will be distracted checking their Blackberry. And the third person will likely show up late and leave early. How are you supposed to have a conversation with three people when two seem like they'd rather be anywhere else? Well, do your best to engage everyone in the conversation and don't assume someone's lack of interest means that you won't get the job (assume it means they have something else work related that is taking bandwidth).

Be serious but have some fun. This is a game after all. Expect it to get tough. Expect the person to be an asshole. Don't take it personally. I recall one interview from my banking days when a tough as nails female colleague of mine and I were interviewing a male MBA candidate. It went something like this:

Banker: "So describe to me how to value a company?"

MBA student: "Well, you can build a discounted cash flow analysis or use comps analysis."

Banker: "Ok. How do you build a DCF?"

MBA student: "You determine cash flows and discount them back to the present day using a discount rate."

Banker: "Right and how do you determine cash flows?"

MBA student: "Well, you take the net change in cash from the company's cash flow statement." (Wrong answer by the way.)

Banker: "What?"

MBA student: "Um you take the net change in cash from…"

Banker: "I heard you the first time. That's not right."

MBA student: "Well that's how we learned in class…"

Banker: "I don't care what you learned in class. That's wrong. Try again."

MBA student: "…..um….ah…I…."

Banker: "Nothing?"

MBA student: "Well we did a project…"

Banker: "I don't care what project you did. It's wrong. I'm not sure what they are teaching you at (MBA school) but

44

I'd ask for my money back. Most undergraduates know this answer and you're in business school? You should have known this answer before business school. Did you forget?"

MBA student: "I guess I'm just getting confused."

Banker: "Confused about what? This is simple. Basic finance 101. I can't believe you don't know this."

MBA student: "Um..I..." (looks down at lap)

Banker: "Free cash flow starts with net income…then what?"

MBA student: "Um…well…" (looks up with watery eyes)

Banker: "Do you know what comes next?"

MBA student: "Um…" (wiping tears from his eyes)

Me: "Ok let's move on."

This person didn't treat it like a game. I have no doubt he really wanted the job, but he took the situation too personally (granted I realize my colleague was a bit out of line). Don't let that be you. By the way, after the fact, my female colleague told the other interviewers that she made "that guy cry" with a bit of joyful guilt. Of course the "sales guy" tried to smooth things over while "the apprehensive" called HR. In case you were wondering, she was an "analytical mind".

Section 3: Acing the Interview

Chapter 6: Types of Questions

So now you're ready to get down to business. Most interviews take a fairly common format and include the following major areas or categories of discussion:
- Softball
- Industry
- Market sizing
- Technical
- Behavioral
- Other
- Q&A

Softball

While the order may sometimes change, the first area of discussion is really around you. This is your story. Your story is framed in softball questions like, "Tell me about yourself?" "Walk me through your resume." "So you want to be an investment banker." These questions appear the easiest, but as discussed previously, they are often the hardest.

Do not assume the person knows your story because you got the interview. It is possible they got your resume the night before and only read it five minutes ago. Just because someone else understood your story, does not mean this person already understands it too. So you will need to start from the beginning, even if it feels like you are repeating yourself. You are and that's ok; every time you tell your story, think of it as another potential evolution and opportunity to improve.

You should be able to answer your story questions in 45 to 60 seconds max. You should know your story so cold that even if interrupted you can quickly go back to the narrative in your head. If it feels rehearsed, it is. If it feels formulaic, it is. But consider the alternative. If you don't have a story, you will not get the offer. Period.

As for the interruptions in your story, they are often looking for clarifying points on your experiences. They could ask, "And what team role did you play on that school project?" Or perhaps, "What was your recommendation and who took action based on your work?" This could also sound like, "What was the outcome of your internship?" What they are attempting to determine is the value you added. They ultimately want to hire someone who is going to add value to their team and their firm. They also want to understand your ability to work on a team, namely their team, so they are trying to determine if you are a team player.

You can often get closer to this "value add" in the way you structure your resume. I often see people make the following mistake:

> *Barclays*
> *Summer Intern (June – August 2014), New York, NY*
> *Assisted M&A deal team with preparation of pitch books and creation of comp sets.*

What the above description is lacking is the value you added. "Assisted, preparation and creation" are great action words, but it lacks an outcome. It begs the question, "What happened as a result?" You can do yourself (and the interviewer) the favor of attempting to answer that on your resume. Something like below is better:

> *Barclays*
>
> *Summer Intern (June – August 2014), New York, NY*
>
> *Assisted M&A deal team with preparation of pitch books, which resulted in two new clients. Managed the creation of comp sets, which were presented to the Board of Directors in a live deal.*

Anything on your resume is fair game by the way. You should be able to go deeper than what it says on paper (again, remember the one page rule). Do not embellish on paper or in person. They will know and they will call you on it. There is nothing worse than someone that tries to lie his or her way into a job. It sets a bad precedent.

Make sure every experience on your resume is positive. Be sure to frame all challenges as growth opportunities. For example, "I didn't get as much as I had hoped out of my internship because my associate was too busy working a few deals and thus was very hands off" could be better framed as, "Given I joined as three deals were in flight, I quickly learned to proactively seek out opportunities to assist."

The interviewer may also take you on tangents on your familiarity with Excel and PowerPoint (Word is easy so no need to mention it). Be prepared to talk about your use of those tools, specifically in how you've grown your skills (no one expects you to be an expert already; they will train you).

Industry

With industry questions, the interviewer is looking to see your general and specific interest in what they do. If they gauge your industry knowledge to be low, they will take it as a sign that you don't want to do what they do.

Questions may sound like, "Tell me three things you read in the Wall St. Journal this week." If you don't know three headlines, what they think is, "Well I guess you're not that interested in finance." While you can cram for this question, it is best to have been reading the financial rags for some time. The interviewer will often want you to go deeper than just the first paragraph of an article. They will often ask you questions that attempt to link different stories together. For example, "What do you think rising interest rates (first article you read) will do to the price of oil (second article you read)?" From having read many articles preceding the interview, you will be able to stitch together a narrative on what is happening in the market. While you may not be right (more on that later), you at least sound interested and that is worth a lot.

The next question they may ask has to do with companies you follow. These questions often sound like,

> "Do you invest and if so which companies?"
> "If I were to give you a million dollars, where would you invest it?"
> "Tell me about a company you follow."
> "If you were CEO for a day, which company would it be and why?"

What they are attempting to get at here is your interest level. Again, if you don't follow any companies or don't have a good thesis for why you would invest in a particular company, then what they hear is that you are not interested in what they do. Don't worry if you don't already invest; it's not a prerequisite but you at least should have some ideas.

I suggest you have two or three companies in your back pocket. You should be familiar with the following:
- Income statement – what is their top and bottom line and growth trends?
- Balance sheet – how much cash and debt and any recent changes?
- Cash flow statement – is it positive or negative and any noteworthy changes?

- Press releases – any recent new product launches or management changes?
- M&A – any recent deals, the rationale, and if they were a part of it?
- Competitive positioning – who are their competitors and what is their competitive advantage?

You should pick a company you feel passionate about. It will come through in the interview. If you like sports, pick Nike or Fitbit, for example. If you like clothes, pick Limited Brands or Lululemon. If you like media and entertainment, pick Netflix or Disney. If you like to eat, pick Chipotle or Taco Bell (Yum Brands). Don't pick a company you find boring because it will come through in the interview and will make for a poor discussion. Also, don't pick a company that they may not have heard of, because they will likely think it a bad choice.

Try to pick a company in the space in which they work. For example, if they are a tech M&A banker, pick a software company. If they are in industrials, pick a manufacturing company. If they are in aviation, pick an airline. Realize that talking about something they know about is risky, since they will know more than you, but I'd err on the side of their interest any day. If you find their industry boring and you can't find an interesting company, then default to what you do find interesting and consider looking for other job opportunities.

You need to be positive in everything you say about the companies. Firstly, you haven't earned the right to be negative. Secondly, it's very possible the person sitting across from you calls that company a client. If you were to elaborate why you think Facebook overpaid for What's App, it's very possible one of those companies was a client and now you basically called them stupid. No job for you. You can frame negatives as opportunities. For example, "Given the $19 billion ($22 billion at close) purchase price for What's App, which had nil revenues, Facebook clearly was willing to take a potential competitor out of the market and bet on their ability to monetize a user similar to on their platform." (Note: At the time of the deal, the valuation of a What's App user (of which there were 450M) was less than that of a Facebook user, so they no doubt felt like they got a deal).

Another way the interviewer may get to your level of industry knowledge is to ask more pointed questions which can get a bit confrontational. Let's take a simple example with Apple's growth rates. Assume the question is, "What do you think Apple will grow at this year?" Well, you happen to know that Apple did $156B in FY'12 (45% year on year growth), $171B in FY'13 (9% YoY) and $183B in FY'14 (7% YoY). So you are likely to believe that Apple is being impacted by the "law of large numbers" which says it gets harder to grow the bigger you get (by the way, Apple grew the equivalent of a Starbucks in FY'13 and four Teslas in FY'14). With just this information, you say, "Given historical trends, it appears Apple is facing the law of large numbers so I think Apple will grow in low single digits, maybe 5-6% next year." Is that a logical answer? Yes. Do you know the answer? No. Does the interviewer know the answer? No. Does anyone know the answer? No. Why? Because last time I checked, no one can tell the future (we'll spend more time on that in the market sizing section). If your interviewer knew the future, they wouldn't be interviewing you; they'd be sitting on a large yacht in a tropical destination picking stocks and beating the market.

This is where things usually get interesting. It's very possible the interviewer may get a bit confrontational. He or she may say something like, "Five or six percent, is that really what you think? Given the tough competition and saturating markets, I'm guessing they fall to negative ten." It makes no difference. If you had said negative 10%, they would probably called out new product releases and high growth geographies, but let's go back to your initial answer and the interviewer's initial response. You now have a choice. You could say (to their negative 10%), "Yeah you're right, I guess I over estimated." I'd suggest not saying that at all. Again, they don't know the future any more than you.

What I would recommend saying is, "I hear what you are saying and while competition is increasing in some geographies, like the U.S., and some products, like the iPod, may be saturating and even cannibalized by other products, the fact that they are launching a new line of iPhones, which currently accounts for more than half of their revenue, gives me reason to believe they will continue to be a growth company." I do believe that the interviewer will respect you for pushing back. After all, this is what they want in an employee. They want someone who is going to think for themselves and come up with logical assumptions about future growth. I don't recommend telling them they are wrong and you are right (recall our Type A discussion), but respectfully counter their argument with data and passion.

If the interviewer had asked you how you came up with five or six percent and you said, "I don't know I guessed," then I suggest you pick up your things and leave. The interview is unofficially over. They don't want to hire someone who is going to guess. Again, I realize the double standard in what I'm saying. Isn't trying to predict the future an inherent guess? Not exactly. As we'll discuss in the next section on market sizing, there is a range of potential right answers. For example, there is no way Apple will grow 100% next year. Not possible. That is a wrong answer.

In addition, it pays to have conviction and confidence in your answer, even though you know you are going to be wrong. They would rather hire someone who is wrong but confident in their analysis than someone who is right but got lucky guessing.

So what did Apple actually grow at in FY'15? Well they jumped to $234 billion, an increase of $50B or roughly 28%. That's right, they grew an entire Disney in a year. Law of large numbers…what's that again? Nobody saw that coming.

Market sizing

Next up is market sizing. One of the core skills of investment banking is valuation. Valuation answers the fundamental question of what something is worth, and valuation is based on growth. Growth is based on market size and the ability for a company to capture a portion of that market, so it is an important topic to discuss.

Let's go back to the Apple growth question. Ultimately Apple's ability to grow is impacted by its ability to 1) capture a certain share of a market (e.g. smartphones), 2) with a particular product or service (e.g. iPhone 6). While this may seem like an insurmountable task, it starts with asking questions like, "How many people could potentially buy an iPhone?" "Which geography or demographics am I measuring?" "What has been the incremental growth in sales for each previous iPhone release?" "How many people bought an iPhone 1-5 and might want to upgrade to a 6?" Hopefully this is providing some insights into how you would answer the question. We'll come back to the answer.

Let's take an "easier" question like, "How many cups of coffee are sold each day in New York City?" What do you think? One million? Ten million? Twenty million? I can assure you that no one (not even the CEO of Starbuck's) knows the answer to that question. The right answer is almost irrelevant. Ultimately what the interviewer cares about is your ability to think logically about the problem and size the market.   You should think about how you are going to address the question (we'll call this your framework) before blurting out an answer. Even if you guess right, the interviewer will ask how you got the answer. Again, it's better to analyze and be wrong than to guess and be right.

While the right answer may not be what the interviewer is judging you on, similar to the Apple growth question, there is a range of potential right answers, which you will be judged on. For example, 100 million cups of coffee is wrong; there is not enough stressed bankers or non-European tourists to generate 100 million cups sold in a day.

Be prepared to take some time (60 seconds max) to think about how you are going to answer the question. You are encouraged to ask clarifying questions like, "Do you mean any coffee product like a Frappuccino or just ground coffee beans and milk?" You shouldn't waste your whole minute asking questions however (note, the consulting case interview often has a similar element where more question asking is encouraged, but in this case you should make some assumptions and move on; the interviewer can correct your assumptions).

I suggest you write down your framework on a piece of paper during those 60 seconds. Don't think about the answer right away or the difficulty of the question. Don't think, "Oh crap, oh crap, oh crap." Think about how you will address the question and start writing it down on paper.

Let's think about two potential frameworks for how you size a market, namely top down and bottom up. The first looks at the whole pie and then slices it accordingly. The second looks at the slices and tries to construct the size of the pie. On your piece of paper, where you are jotting down your framework, you might start with a simple arrow up or down to get your mind in the respective mentality. Let's look at each framework more closely.

As mentioned, top down market sizing starts with a big number and parses it down to a smaller share. It usually takes the shape of something like:

(%Population) x (% Product) x (% Time) x (% Company)= Share of Revenue

It makes sense to think of some common numbers when doing a top down analysis, like the number of people in a particular country (e.g. 320 million in the U.S) or the percentage of a population that is a certain age (recall the bell curve from high school math). It's important you are directionally correct versus exact; for example, if you used 300 million people in the U.S., you'd likely not be criticized.

Let's apply the top down market sizing methodology to the coffee question. On your piece of paper you should have drawn an arrow pointing down. You might have then jotted down, from top to bottom, things like:

1) number of people (living and working) in New York City,
2) % of people of coffee drinking age,
3) % of those people that drink coffee,
4) average number of cups of coffee consumed daily,
5) % of those people that buy vs. make coffee,

Next to each element of your framework, you would jot down some assumptions, until you have an analysis that looks like the following:
- (# of people) – define scope as Manhattan's 1.6 million residents and 1.5 million commuters or 3.1 million people (source: U.S. Census); note this number is much smaller than the estimated 10 million who are in New York City, which is a scope question you can ask
- x (coffee drinking age) – assume age demographics puts 80% of population as coffee buying age of 18-80 (source: US census)
- x (drink coffee) – of the 80%, assume 50% drink coffee (source: family/friends insight) or 3.1 million x 80% x 50% = 1.24 million coffee drinkers
- x (units) – assume that the average coffee drinker drinks two cups of coffee per day (source: family/friends insight)
- x (buy vs. make) – half of the residents and non-residents probably make a cup of coffee at home (defining as not sold), then on average, 1.24 million coffee drinkers x 1 cup + 1.24 million coffee drinkers * (50% not brewing at home) = 1.86 million cups of coffee

Here is another top down answer:

- (Population) – define population as size of restaurant industry in United States or $709 billion in annual sales (source: National Restaurant Association); if you didn't know this number you might have guessed $200 a month for 320 million people
- x (% of Population) – define % of population as Manhattan's 1.6 million residents and 1.5 million commuters or 3.1 million people (roughly 1% of 320 million people in US (source: U.S. Census), so 1% of US restaurant industry sales = $6.87 billion in yearly Manhattan restaurant sales, not accounting for the cost of NYC, which is roughly 1.5x more expensive (based on per diem rates of $71 in NYC vs. $46 in St. Louis; source: U.S. GSA), and factoring in 260 weekdays in the year (notice I didn't use 365, but I could have), daily sales = $6.8 billion / 260 x 1.5 = $40.8 million
- x (% Product) – of the % of coffee vs. non-coffee restaurant sales, take an average of 2 cups of coffee per day (source: family/friends insight), where a cup of coffee is $4, and divide by the per diem of $71 to get 11% of daily restaurant sales or $4.6 million in daily

coffee sales; note assuming non-coffee drinkers are compensated for by power drinkers
- x (% Company) – if we were looking at a share of wallet, then we could break it down by chain (e.g. Starbucks vs. Dunkin' Donuts vs. independent chains)
- = Share of Revenue – since we're looking at 100% of all retail stores = $4.60 million in coffee sold each weekday in Manhattan (at $4/cup = 1.15 million cups)

In a bottoms up market sizing analysis, you start with something small and work your way up to the larger number. It usually takes the shape of something like:

(# of Customers) x (Units) x (Price / Unit) x (Duration) = Total Revenue

On your piece of paper you should have drawn an arrow pointing up. You might have then jotted down, from top to bottom, things like:
1) number of coffee serving locations on a block in Manhattan,
2) number of blocks in Manhattan,
3) number of people frequenting a coffee shop or restaurant per hour,
4) number of hours the coffee shop or restaurant is open,

5) number of cups of coffee consumed by each person,

Again, next to each you would start jotting down some assumptions, until you have an analysis that looks like the following:

- (# of Coffee Shops) – 3 per square block (source: estimate based on walking through Manhattan)
- x (number of blocks in Manhattan) – Manhattan is about 200 streets long by 10 streets wide or 2,000 blocks (source: estimate from viewing a map)
- x (# of Customers) – assume one customer every 4 minutes in a coffee shop or 15 per hour on average
- x (# of Hours) – assume the coffee shops are open from 6am to 9pm or 15 hours (source: my local Starbucks)
- x (Purchase) – assume each person buys only one cup of coffee (which should also account for those people that sit there all day and "work")
- = 1.35 million cups of coffee sold each weekday in Manhattan

You will notice we got a range of potential answers. That is ok. Ideally both methods should be within an order of magnitude of each other. Ultimately the different answers we got are based on the different assumptions we used. It is worth identifying the assumptions that can create the greatest variance (this is called a sensitivity analysis). Also it is often worth spot-checking your assumptions with a known variable. Ultimately while the "right answer" is preferred, the thought process is most valuable.

Often times these market-sizing questions are meant to get you to think about growth opportunities. For example, in an interview I was once asked, "Should a hotel chain put in Wi-Fi?" This required me to size the opportunity, specifically (occupancy rate) x (days in year) x (average length of stay for business or pleasure travel) x (daily price for Wi-Fi) = Total Revenue. I then compared that to the cost of installing and operating the Wi-Fi in a discounted cash flow analysis to get a return on investment (more on DCFs later).

Here are some other esoteric "market sizing" questions I've received or given which should get you thinking:
- How many windows in Manhattan?
    You might approach this in a bottom's up fashion by using the square block calculation, but this time accounting for a third dimension of height.
- How many golf balls fit in an airplane?

You might approach this also bottoms up by taking a circumference of golf ball and compare that to the circumference of a jet.

- How much does the earth weigh?
Again, you might approach by taking a small portion of the earth (core, mantle, crust, water, rock, human elements, etc.) and expanding that to the whole.

So let's turn back to Apple. The question remains what would the iPhone 6 impact be to Apple's top line in FY15. For reference, they sold $102B of iPhones in FY14 and $91B in FY13. You can quickly do the math to apply the FY13 to FY14 growth rate of 12% to get $114B in FY15. You'd be justified in your answer but you'd be wrong.

Assume they grow market share by 10% in the US (30 million units) and 2.5% in China (32.5 million units). That would equal another 62.5 million phones in two growth markets and at an average sale price of $650, sales would grow by $41B (40%) for a total of $143B. Closer. Maybe you factor in other growth markets like the rest of Asia Pacific. Or maybe you account for a slightly higher ASP in the refresh rate for older iPhones. The actual growth was $53B or 52%. Yes, Apple's iPhone business alone grew approximately thirteen whole Chipotles (the company, not your local restaurant) in one year.

Technical

Now on to a topic that causes much stress. Let's get something out of the way right now. You don't need to know the answer to every technical question to get the job. I hope that puts you somewhat at ease.

You should take this section of questions seriously however. If you don't know the answer to more than one question, you're likely not going to get the job. What they hear is someone who hasn't put in the work and likely doesn't want to do the job.

If you're an undergrad and you get a question that you don't know the answer to, then you can politely respond, "I'm sorry, I don't know the answer to that question. It's not something we covered at (name your school)." That's right, I'm telling you to blame your school. It has broad shoulders and can take it. I'm not one that likes to point fingers, but in this situation, it is usually the best option.

For the MBAs reading this, you can try the same approach, but be prepared for some pushback especially if that person went to your school. You (as well as the undergrads) can try to ask for clarifying information like, "Can I clarify that what I think you're asking is..." If they want to give you more information then they will. If they say, "Not important, let's move on," then I suggest you do that as well. Don't ruminate in your head about missing a question and that the interview is likely over and you failed. Again, it's not true.

Here's what you should absolutely not do: guess. If you guess and get it wrong you will not get the job. Full stop. Do not pass go. Do not collect $200. No job for you. And guessing usually involves lots of embarrassment on your part. It often goes something like this:

> Interviewer: "What is Beta and why and how do you delever it?"
> You: "Ok. A beta is the riskiness of a stock relative to the market." (note: try not to sound like a robot when you read back something you've memorized)
> Interviewer: "Right."
> You: "And you delever the Beta when it is for a private company." (note: wrong answer by the way)
> Interviewer: "How so?"
> You: "Right, well because it is a private company you need to take its Beta and compare it to other public companies." (note: digging the hole deeper)
> Interviewer: "I see. And how would you do that?"

You: "Well you take the private company's Beta and weight it based on the company's market cap relative to other public companies." (note: still digging)

Interviewer: "And how do you do that?"

You: "Right, so you compare the public companies' debt to equity weighting relative to your company to get a percentage, then you take that percentage and average across all the comparable companies then multiply by your company's beta." (note: you just keep digging)

Interviewer: "And you get a bigger or smaller number?"

You: "Well it depends on how many companies you use." (note: in for a penny in for a pound)

Interviewer: "Do you have any idea what you are talking about?"

You: "Yes, I mean…well the Beta is usually larger since you usually have more companies."

Interviewer: "No. You started out ok but the last few answers were wrong."

You: "I think I may have mixed up the math a bit on the calculation." (note: you should shut up now)

Interviewer: "Actually, a private company doesn't have a Beta. That's what you are trying to find. So basically everything you said after that was wrong too."

You: "Oh." (note: no job for you; put down the shovel)

I'll use the analogy of fishing here. If you've ever fished, you know that sometimes you let the fish take the bait and run with it a little. Then you yank back hard to let the hook set in the fish's mouth. That feeling of letting you run with the answer then calling B.S. is fun for the banker, but not so fun for you. You'll have a tendency to keep going but eventually they are going to cause you pain. It would have been easier to blame your school.

The questions you will field in this section are fairly standard questions but bankers will take different approaches. Some like to start high level and get into the details:

> Question 1: "How do you value a company?"
> Question 2: "Walk me through how to do a DCF."
> Question 3: "What is the formula for WACC?"
> Question 4: "How do you calculate the cost of equity?"
> Question 5: "When might you delever a company's Beta?"

Other interviewers may jump around a bit:

> Question 1: "What is working capital?"
> Question 2: "What are some commonly used financial ratios?"
> Question 3: "What is the present value formula?"
> Question 4: "Describe to me how to do comps analysis."
> Question 5: "Which costs more, debt or equity?"

Other interviewers may focus the majority of the discussion on technical questions (guess which type they are) while others may not ask you a single technical question. Some interviewers may ask you concepts while others may ask you formulas. Some interviewers may hand you a financial statement and ask you a question, though most will not. At no time will anyone hand you a computer and have you solve something. First, there likely won't be enough time and second they don't want you on their computer. The only finance job where you are asked to solve models is private equity, so if you are interviewing at PE shops, be prepared to solve a "paper LBO". A paper LBO is outside the scope of this book, but basically you are buying something for X and reselling for Y, hoping to make a high return while able to pay off higher debt levels.

Some additional technical questions include:
- How do the three financial statements relate?
- What is an accounting ratio used for and give an example?
- What is equity vs. enterprise value?
- How do you do a discounted cash flow analysis?
- How do you do comps?
- How can two companies with the same enterprise value be trading at different P/E multiples?

- You buy a piece of machinery for $100. Walk me through the impact to the income statement, balance sheet and cash flow statement.

Many more example technical questions can be found online, in your school's career center, and by attending class and seminars.

Behavioral:

Behavioral questions are meant to see how you respond to some challenging questions about dealing with certain situations or people. It's meant to see if you are capable of being a part of the team.

- Leadership & team work:
  You may get a question or two that is meant to gauge your experience working with or leading teams. For example, "Tell me about a team project you worked on at school, your role, and the outcome." You should stress the value you added to the team and your influence on the outcome. If they ask, "Tell me about a time you decided it was better to follow than lead," then I'd again stress the value you added to the team and the outcome. Or if they ask, "In your internship last summer, tell me about your role on the team." Again, I'd stress the value

you added to the team and the outcome. Do you get the picture?

- Hard work:

    You may get a question or two which attempt to gauge your willingness and understanding of what you are getting yourself into by becoming an investment banker. You should have a good answer for, "Why do you want to work 100 hours a week?" Only you can answer that question, but it should not be about money. You may also get a question like, "It's your brother/sister's wedding this weekend but I need you in the office working a deal. What would you do?" What a horrible question to ask you. You just met them and they are already asking you to choose between work and family. I can assure you the wrong answer is, "Sorry I'm going to the wedding." Believe it or not, the wrong answer is also, "I'll skip the wedding; we're not that close anyway." The right answer is a combination of both, "I'll skip the rehearsal dinner, be working from the bathroom during the slow songs, and be on the first flight back once the cake is cut." I mean it is your sibling after all. You can choose to not have a life after you start in the job.

- Greatest strengths and weaknesses:

These are tough questions and it may feel formulaic to answer but you should be able to answer them without thinking. As for strengths, it pays to play up things like drive, work ethic, good attitude, teamwork, leadership, attention to detail, ability to handle pressure, self-discipline, communication skills, etc. Similarly for weaknesses, it also pays to play up those same things. How is that possible? "One of my greatest weaknesses is I get so involved in tasks at hand that I sometimes fail to see the bigger picture. A good example of this was a school project where I ended up pulling an all nighter not having realized the deadline got pushed back a few days." What this says to the interviewer is that you are a hard worker and that they can help you see the forest through the trees. I'd stay away from being brutally honest, for example, "I'm a complete slob," will likely not help your job prospects.

- Other behavioral questions:
    o Ability to solve problems
    o Ability to reflect good values
    o Ability to communicate effectively
    o Ability to work with clients / interpersonal skills
    o Ability to adapt to changing situations
    o Ability to manage your and other's time

- Ability to self motivate and take initiative
- Ability to handle stress and pressure

Other:

There are other potential questions you may get asked. Here are some question types, in no particular order:
- Writing test:
Contrary to popular belief, you do a lot of writing in banking. On my first day as an associate, my MD James handed me a copy of <u>The Elements of Style</u>, by Strunk and White, with a bit of advice to, "Read this and follow it." I used to give these tests often and I know they are still done today at many top banks. What this looks like is the interviewer walking into the conference room and dropping a newspaper, notebooks and pens on the conference table. He or she says, "Pick an article and summarize it. You have 60 minutes. I'll be back to collect them. Any questions? Ok, go." Now what are they looking for in such a test? First, that you can communicate in English (or whatever the bank's native language) and second that you can form a logically structured argument. Now is when things get interesting. First you see a lot of nicely dressed people fighting over one newspaper (teamwork). Next, after reading your article and perhaps

exchanging for another, you should jot down an outline (planning). You won't have the benefit of cutting and pasting, so framing up your paper in advance is a good idea. Also, if you haven't written by hand in a while, you will soon realize that it hurts (endurance). You will notice a lot of your fellow interviewees trying to shake the pain away, but the clock keeps ticking (deadlines). What most people do is just start writing and then cross things out. Some draw arrows to other pages. I've even seen interviewees try to physically cut and paste using tape they may have scrounged up. So what you turn in is a messy product (presentation). While it may be the best-written argument in the bunch, the perception is that you don't do quality work. I'm not saying this will prevent you from getting the job, but it certainly doesn't help your cause. Turn in a concise, well written, and professional looking product and you should be fine.

- Trick questions:
Sometimes the interviewers will ask you questions that don't have an answer. They want to see how you respond. They want to see if your face turns red. They want to see if you start to perspire. They want to see your body language. They want to see how long it takes you to give up and how many wrong answers you give

before hand. Here's an example I know all too well from an interview with a bulge bracket bank:

> Interviewer: "A car goes around a one mile track and it takes 60 seconds. How fast does it need to go on its next lap to double its average speed?" (note: he had just asked me how much the Earth weighed; I (recalling high school Physics) had responded, "Well technically the Earth doesn't weigh anything." The interviewer turned his head sideways (there's that damn dog look again) and asked me, "Well, what is the mass of the Earth?" I knocked it out of the park.
> Me: "120 miles per hour." (blurting out the first thought that came to mind)
> Interviewer: "No."
> Me: "Ok, let me take a second and think about it." (looking up at the ceiling and noticing it is getting kind of hot...I think I might have even started using fingers to count just to look like I was taking it seriously)
> Interviewer: "Do you need a piece of paper?"
> Me: "Yes, please." (note: always bring paper to an interview; staring at the blank piece of paper I now noticed how tight my tie was; at this point I had drawn two tracks on the piece of paper; as I

looked up the interviewer had his arms crossed and was just staring at me with no expression.)

Me: "240 mph?"

Interviewer: "Are you guessing?"

Me: (thinking to myself) "Isn't that obvious?" (but actually answering) "I'm having difficulty with the calculation." (now realizing the sun was beating down on me and I was wiping sweat off my brow)

Interviewer: "Do you need a calculator?"

Me: "Yes please." (note: always bring a calculator to an interview; at this point while I'm pecking away on his calculator, he actually started checking his email and typing away on his keyboard; I think I let that go on another minute or so, which felt like much longer)

Me: "I'm having a hard time finding an answer."

Interviewer (without looking up from his computer): "That's because there is no answer. You can't double your average speed."

Me: (trying to save face) "Ah, that's probably why I couldn't find an answer."

In this case the interviewer wanted to see how I handled stress. I failed and as you might imagine I didn't get the job. If you are wondering if this is just some sick joy seeking sport for the interviewer, you are partially right.

The real (main?) reason they ask questions like this is because they deal with situations where they don't know the answer and an irate client is demanding the answer. They want to see how you respond. Do you get visibly uncomfortable? If so, you'll likely do that in the real world as well. I left thinking that the stupid question with no answer had zero bearing on my capability as a banker, but it did.

- World news:
I've known interviewers who would do world news test. Personally I was never a fan, but it is basically another way to see if you follow current events (in this case not always financial). The banker turned movie producer used to quiz people on foreign leaders in the news with questions like, "Name the leaders of Afghanistan, Israel and Mexico." She was a bit sadistic and would actually ask people about geography ("What is the capital of New Hampshire?") and even presidents ("Name as many presidents as you can, preferably in chronological order."). Crazy I know, but remember it is a stress test. How are you going to respond?

- The last xyz:

If they ask you the last book you read, have a good answer to that. Don't say 50 Shades of Grey. There is no follow-up question to that, except for maybe "How do you delever a company's Beta?" It should be a book that you can have a conversation about. It doesn't have to be an autobiography or a financial story, but those do help. That goes for movies, music albums, apps, etc. Try to make your answer intellectually stimulating so that you can have a conversation about it.

- About you:
  At the bottom of your resume, there should be a section on your skills and interests. You want to have a conversation about these things. This is the aforementioned airport test. If you put down skiing, be prepared to talk about the last place you skied. If you like running, be prepared to talk about races you've run. If you like hiking, be prepared to talk about the last place you hiked. If you like golf, what's your handicap? Ideally the interviewer does one of those things as well, so now you're having a conversations about Jackson Hole or the Master's and that is a good thing. Now you've developed a personal bond.

I once had an interview where the MD and I talked about baseball for an hour (he was a Yankees fan and I a Red Sox fan), including going outside the office while he took a smoke break (3 cigarettes actually) and drank a quad from Starbucks (that's four shots, which I didn't even know existed at the time; I'd soon learn). Needless to say I got the job offer and I knew it as the meeting wrapped up.

If you are not prepared to talk about those things on your resume, it will raise a red flag. If they ask, "Where do you go skiing," and you answer, "Well actually I haven't been in a few years," then they are going to look at you like, "Then why put it on your resume?" You've lost an opportunity to establish a personal connection with the interviewer and now they are questioning what else you've embellished on your resume.

- Other jobs:
If they ask you what other jobs you are interested in or applying for, you should have a good answer. You are young and your whole career is ahead of you, so you should be looking at other things. Ultimately you should have a good answer for why you want to do investment banking more than consulting, law, strategy, etc. If they

ask you if you have any offers in hand, you should mention them, even if they are not in banking. It's nice to be wanted and generally the more someone wants you the more others will want you (applies to dating too). What you shouldn't do is volunteer the exploding offers without being asked. It will likely come across as a bit conceited when you say, "So I have an offer from McKinsey, so can you let me know when I will find out if I got this job?" Cocky. No job for you.

Q&A

"So what questions do you have for me?" Sounds simple enough right? Guess what? It's also a test. Don't say, "No I've taken enough of your time. I don't have any questions." If they didn't want to answer questions they wouldn't have asked. This is often their attempt to sell you on the bank after you've passed the other questions. Let them sell.

Nerves will often get the best of you so make sure you have memorized the questions you are going to ask. Don't look in your notebook and read them off.

Don't ask them anything that you can research and find the answer to fairly quickly. I've had bankers say to me, "You can find that on our website. Next question." It shows you didn't do the work and that you're wasting their time.

Don't ask philosophical questions about their life choices like, "Any regrets in choosing the path you did?" I'm sure they have lots, but they are none of your business, especially when you are interviewing for the first step on their path.

Don't worry about asking the same question to multiple interviewers. They are not going to sit down later and cross-reference questions you asked. "Holy shit, that bastard asked me the same exact question." Really? No. If anything, listen for the answers that different people give to the same question. If they are wildly different, be concerned as someone is likely being less than honest.

Ask them questions about the process. When will you expect to hear back? Ask them questions about how one evolves in the role to take on more responsibility. I know it sounds cliché but you're expressing value that you will add before you even have the job. Ask them about opportunities to work overseas. Ask them about your ability to improve existing processes. Ask them about formal training programs. Ask them about informal mentorship opportunities. Ask them questions that make it seem like you are eager to grow in the role and add value.

Chapter 7: To Do's and Not To Do's

In summary, there are some things you should and shouldn't do in an interview. First the to do's:
- Show up on time (or preferably early, but not too early...usually 10 to 15 minutes before is when you want to start getting through security).
- Dress the part (I, like Oscar Wilde, believe you can never be overdressed or overeducated, but there are some that say no flashy, expensive ties until you've earned it). Get yourself a decent pair of shoes. They are a good investment and you will have them for a long time. I've had many an interviewer not so casually look at my shoes.

- Always be nice to the person at the front desk. They have a hard job and deserve your respect, also they may have the ear of one (or more) of the hiring managers.
- Be prepared to wait (and make sure you look busy).
- Be energetic and excited to be there, but also talk slowly and clearly; no robots.
- Look the interviewer in the eyes even if they are distracted.
- Be confident but not cocky.
- Recite your story in 45 to 60 seconds max.
- Be prepared to talk in detail about everything on your resume.
- Be positive about all experiences you've had even if they weren't positive.
- Have your thinking cap on and remember they care more about how you think than the answer you get right or wrong.
- Be prepared for the tough questions and be ready to be made to feel uncomfortable.
- Ask the interviewer if they know the timeline for getting back to you (again, show excitement but not cockiness).
- Follow-up with a thank you note. If possible, reference something from your conversation (e.g. skiing Jackson Hole) as it will help them remember you from the many other people they have interviewed. While I prefer a

hand-written thank you note, email has become acceptable these days. You may want to ask the interviewer for a business card (again, no *American Psycho* jokes) so you have their email address.

Now the not to do's

- Don't be too friendly with the other interviewees.
- Don't forget your resume, notebook, pen or calculator.
- Don't ever mention how long the interviews are taking and don't ask to reschedule anything for travel reasons.
- Don't give any non-public information (e.g. the buyer in a deal) from an internship (you can tell them that that information has not been made public yet and they will back off; there is no risk to you; if anything they will respect you for it).
- Don't get frustrated or lose your cool.
- Don't think you blew the interview if the interviewer is being a prick (he or she may just be a prick or may be having a bad day).
- Don't talk too fast or sound robotic if you are nervous.
- Don't look like you are bored or are not busy.
- Don't be somebody that you're not.

Section 4: Post Interview

Chapter 8: Careful what you wish for

I hired someone once out of an Ivy League school who ticked all the boxes. He was an Econ major with a high GPA who came from a family of bankers. He said all the right things about why he wanted to work in finance. The person lasted all of fourteen days before coming into the office one Monday morning (in a full suit) and quitting. I had actually blown him off for about two hours while fighting a fire. I can only imagine what was going through his mind during those two hours. When he came into my office the conversation went something like this:

>John: "I don't think I can do this any more."
>Me: "Well it's been a tough two weeks and I know you put in many hours this weekend but it will get better."
>John: "I just can't see myself doing this the rest of my life."

Me: "Why don't you take the rest of the day off and think about it."

John: "Ah, no, I don't think so. I've talked to my parents and they support my decision."

Me: "Ok, well maybe you want to talk with James…he's been doing this a long time and might provide you some comfort."

John: "Ok, I guess but I don't think that will change anything."

Me: "Let me see if he's available. Can you hang on a bit in here?"

John: "Sure."

Me: (returning after a few minutes) "It looks like he's on the phone. Why don't we go grab a coffee and he can come join us."

John: "Actually, I think I'd rather just leave." (note: time kills all deals)

Me: "Ok we can talk more tomorrow…"

John: "No, I mean leave for good. (stands to open the door) I'm just going to go say good-bye to the guys."

Me: "Actually I don't think that's a good idea. Let me walk you to the front door. Sleep on it and if you change your mind please call me tomorrow. We all have bad days."

John: "Ok, thanks."

Me: "Hey John." (as he's walking towards the elevator)

John: "Yeah?"

Me: "I need your badge. Thanks and good luck to you."

Last year I helped place a few people at Goldman Sachs (1% of their incoming i-banking analysts, by my count). This year at least one of them no longer works there, by their choosing. I know what you're thinking and you're right, you might have been more deserving of the job.

To quote Mike Tyson, "Everyone has a plan until you get punched in the mouth." For many, working at an investment bank is like getting punched in the mouth daily. So be careful what you wish for because it may not be all that you ever wanted.

During the time I've been writing this book, there have been many highly publicized suicides in i-banking. At the risk of oversimplifying what are certainly complex issues, let me attempt to keep this on a single plane. Many top students work their butts off for years to obtain the most prestigious finance jobs only to find it is not the panacea they had envisioned. This creates an internal conflict when your job (or firm) is a large portion of how you define yourself. This internal discourse can lead to feelings of hopelessness or of being trapped. As an admitted workaholic, far be it from me to judge others who derive an inordinate amount of self-importance from their job. At the end of the day, no job is worth your life. A job does not define you. You define you.

Chapter 9: You got the job

Congratulations! It surely wasn't easy. You put in the work and should pat yourself on the back. Enjoy the rest of school or whatever job you are in now. Soon your life will be completely consumed by your new job.

For the incoming analyst and associate classes, there is usually a three to four or more week training program at the bank's headquarters. This is a not so gradual indoctrination into the i-banking lifestyle. The days are usually shorter than usual, but you're given lots of homework, sometimes coupled with actual projects your new bosses are managing. You should take this time to get to know your colleagues. You will make some friends for life in those short few weeks.

At the same time, you should take these training weeks very seriously. Your fellow trainees are looking for weaknesses, which they may one day use against you. Your managers are also looking for weaknesses that they hope to shore up before putting you full-time in the line of fire. Having taught many such sessions, I notice people are often afraid to ask questions in fear that it will make them appear weak. Make no mistake this is the time to ask questions. Once you are in the job, your questions won't get as friendly a reception. Learning is not a weakness but being afraid to ask questions is.

While completing training, you are also adapting to the i-banking lifestyle. Office hours increase and free time decreases. Calories increase and exercise decreases. Work increases and hobbies decrease. Time with colleagues increases and time with friends and family decreases.

Nobody will ever tell you to work less in your new role, so it's up to you to manage your work life balance. Many incoming employees feel that if they are not at their desk when a senior person comes by they will not get a large end of year bonus. In isolated instances this is complete nonsense. In aggregate, it is absolutely true. So how do you manage that double standard? Well, nobody can but you.

This can often cause one's outlook on the job and life in general to turn a bit sour. In a way you feel trapped, leading to feelings of misery. Rest assured, you are not alone, and in spite of the challenges, the highs usually outweigh the lows.

Many new employees put on a lot of weight their first year. Think of it as the freshman fifteen only this time you're wearing a suit. This is because you sit at your desk all day while food is brought in to you along with highly caffeinated sugary drinks, provided of course, to keep your energy level high. Combine that with your now decreased time for some of the things you used to do like exercising, sleeping, etc. and the pounds accumulate.

How do you manage both work and life? It's hard but again, only you can do it. If you want to go see a friend for dinner, do it. Just be prepared to get called back to the office which means you're leaving dinner early and picking up the check. If you want to schedule a weekend away with your significant other then do it, just be prepared for some last minute cancellations, maybe even sending a stand-in in your place, and of course, footing the bill. If you want to exercise then do it just be prepared to be interrupted and take a call from the treadmill. I had analysts who worked for me who would announce at 7pm they were going out for a run. They'd be back at their desk by 8:30pm to work a few more hours. Do whatever you can to manage a work and life balance, just make sure you do it.

Chapter 10: You didn't get the job

Through the entire process the hiring manager is looking for ways to weed people out, so odds are you will get dinged. How do I know that? It is a numbers game and there are literally hundreds of people applying for every one banking job so the odds are you won't make the cut at some point. You shouldn't think about it as someone else being more qualified, but rather they made it over all of the hurdles while you tripped on one (or more).

If you've been paying attention, at no point did the process outlined in this book test your qualifications. Therefore, rejection should not ever be considered a statement as to your ability (or inability) to do the job. Nothing could be further from the truth. How do I know? The bank will train everyone they hire for a few weeks upon starting and I can assure you there are no special exceptions for anyone (meaning everyone is assumed to know the same, which is very little). Get those rejection generated thoughts of being unqualified out of your mind.

Maybe you didn't make it past the initial HR screen because you have a low GPA. Don't give up. Countless people were in your shoes at one point and now hold an i-banking job. Your GPA is not an indication of your i-banking aptitude. Attention liberal arts majors who think you got dinged because of your major; while it may not always help (all things being equal relative to another candidate) it's simply not true that your major is the reason you didn't get the job. So keep trying.

If not qualifications, what was measured? First and foremost was your story. If you did not convince everyone why you wanted to do banking then you didn't make the cut. You need to refine your story or the results will remain the same. Your story is measured at all stages of the process. Think back to the asshole of a hiring manager (me) who you first met in Chapter 1 and you will realize it is a numbers game, with me giving your entire life to date a 60 second story check. If you didn't pass that test, then keep refining your story. By the way, we'll come back to how to circumvent me.

Next up we measured your general understanding of the finance industry. Again, this is made sure your interests were aligned with your story. If you failed that test, you need to dive head first into all things finance industry related. While you can cram and sound smart, a person who has been doing this for years will shine head and shoulders above you. If you couldn't answer their questions, go back and get smarter on finance; there is no shortage of information available at your fingertips (Note: if you find yourself not liking this process, then perhaps you should consider another career, because it will only increase).

We then asked you some questions which tested your logical thinking abilities in the context of the job as well as some technical questions which tested your ability to memorize and internalize some fundamental concepts. These questions are also meant to weed people out today. They are not designed to assess your ability to do the job in the future. Again you will be trained on modeling and accounting.

Lastly we threw you some stress related curveballs, which might give a reason to ding you. Turn in a poorly written article synopsis, break under the pressure of us blatantly making you feel uncomfortable or fail my airport test and I'll gladly make the decision process easier by eliminating one more person. Again, you need to practice.

If you didn't get the job, keep trying. When you hear "No" let your mind think "Next Opportunity". If you hear "Fail" let your mouth say "First Attempt at Initial Learning". Cheesy? I don't care. Whatever you do, do not give up. I've known many a friend and classmate who said, "Well I guess I'm not cut out to do this job." Again, nothing could be further from the truth.

Maybe you recently decided you want to do i-banking and your story is not as strong as others. That's ok; it just means you need to work harder than the others. You may need to find an advocate who is going to vouch for you and shepherd you in the process.

So let's go back to that asshole of a hiring manager (me) who is skimming through a stack of 200 resumes late one evening. I may get a knock on the door and someone will enter with your resume in hand and say, "I want to bring this person in." I will take your resume from him or her and put it in the YES pile. It's that easy. You've just cleared the biggest hurdle. Your foot is now in the door.

I realize that easy is a relative term. In fact, finding an advocate within a bank can be quite challenging. It requires cold calling people, many of whom will answer the phone with, "I'm busy, what do you want?" It requires emailing people who you know will likely not reply. It means finding friends of friends or family who know someone who might talk to you. It involves asking for help (without actually asking for help).

Networking can be a challenging process. The lack of replies and the "no's" are often internalized as failures, when they should be perceived as the person being too busy or too much of an asshole to give you their time. If you keep trying, you will eventually find someone who is willing to talk (notice I didn't say help). I know this because most people like to talk about themselves.

If you cold-call someone and say, "Hi, I'm Sally from Stanford and I would like to talk to you about getting a job in i-banking," what they hear is, "this annoying person wants me to help them get a job." Click. That is not their job, so they will not help.

Your goal is to have a dialog with people in the industry such that they may be inclined to help you. If you cold-call someone and say, "Hi I'm Hal from Harvard and I'm interested in learning more about what you do," what they hear is, "this industrious person is trying to get smart about my field. Who knows my field better than me? I can tell them a few things."

Ask the person to meet for a coffee to talk informally about their career progression, or to provide advice to someone in your shoes. Ask the person your questions about the different jobs you are considering and if they have a perspective. Ask the person if there are things they would have done differently or sooner or later during their professional progression. Ask the person if they are willing to speak again as you continue to explore your options and get more insight into their field. Ask the person if they know someone who may be good to talk to next. No matter how long or how many times you speak to someone, you should never ask them to help you get a job.

Do your homework before going to talk to a networking contact. Their time is valuable so don't waste it. Be prepared, practice your pitch, don't talk too much about yourself and take notes.

Additional networking questions you can ask include:
- State of the industry – what are their views on the field of investment banking?
- Skills and expertise – can they compare your credentials to others entering the profession and give advice for improvement?
- Fit – how does one's background and personal attributes contribute to success in the role?

- About the role – what is typical/good/challenging/rewarding/etc. about their job?
- Sources of additional information – what can you read or learn that will help you get smarter?

Ideally by getting to know someone through these informational interviews, they will want to help you. They will become your advocate because they like you, and that person will literally hand deliver you to me.

If you received a rejection during the formal process a bank ran, don't give up. Although the front door may be shut, there is still the back door. So if you do get a rejection, keep banging on doors in search of that advocate. Don't worry about your school or the bank getting upset that you are still trying. Nobody, and I mean nobody will say, "Sorry, you already tried before and we said no." In most banks, the left hand does not know what the right hand is doing, so you have zero risk. As for the schools, you are soon to be a benefactor, so they don't want to scold you. Really, what's the worst anyone can say to you? "No." They've already done that. Keep trying until you get a "yes." That "yes" will change your life forever.

Chapter 11: Closing

That which is worthwhile rarely is easy. Investment banking is no exception. Hopefully this book has provided you with some structure, which can make the process of becoming a successful i-banker easier for you.

You are now on a path that will change your life forever, hopefully for the better. I look back on my many years of banking with great joy, pride in my accomplishments, and growth in my failures. I've met great friend, great leaders, and great people in the industry. I've gone on to do many things in my career as a result of having been an i-banker which I don't think I would have otherwise.

Through stories and language I attempted to convey what the atmosphere and culture of an investment bank are like. Now multiply that by two or three. You can read a car review but it's nothing like going for a test drive. If you find you don't like the car, don't buy it. Life is too short. There are many other careers where you might enjoy yourself more and that is ok.

At the very least, I hope you have learned more about yourself in the process. The skills conveyed in this book apply to life, which is filled with challenges and chances to make a good first impression. What is your story?

I'm very fortunate for the many people that helped me along the way. I hope you too can one day return the favor to others looking to get into the greatest of careers or simply help them find their story. All the best to you.

Chapter 12: Q&A

I've received the below questions countless times (in some form or another) over the past few years from many different people. Here are my answers:

1) I think I want to be an i-banker but can't see myself doing it for more than a year or two. Is it ok to go into it knowing I won't be there for the long run?

    My first inclination is to ask that person why they are already limiting themselves. To me, there is something in your mind saying that you don't really want to be a banker so you construct an out. It's kind of like going out for a run but telling yourself you are going to stop after thirty minutes.

If that helps you lace up your shoes and get out the door then do it, but you might find yourself enjoying the run. So do it if it works for you, but also ask yourself why you are already making excuses. Whatever you do, don't tell the prospective bank that you will only be there for a short time. While odds are that is true, it is not a message you want to convey in your story.

2) What's the most difficult or most uncomfortable interview you ever participated in?

I wish I could say that one stands out for me, but at the end of the day, they were all fairly formulaic. I did have one interview at a European bank based in NYC where the MD was legendary and went by one name (like Prince). My first interviewer was still drunk from the night before. You have to picture a 275 lb. former Yale football player who rolls in 30 minutes late to an 8am interview still reeking of booze, wearing clothes I can only presume are from yesterday, and who is barely able to focus his eyes on me (I'm pretty sure he still had a room spinning problem). I decided to go with the Gordon Gekko approach in the interview and when he asked why I wanted to work there I said something like, "To make fucking money." He smiled at my response. Seeing I was appealing to his drunken side, I went big. I started saying things like, "If you hire me, I will fucking make this bank millions." He might have stood up and cheered at that point. I was fired up too. Unfortunately, I took that same "Greed is good" attitude into the interview with the one named MD and he didn't appreciate my exuberance. I didn't get the job. One of my more reserved classmates did get the internship, but didn't make it past the summer.

Now, as for my most uncomfortable interview, which was also semi- finance related, it involved my first meeting with my future (now former) father-in-law, a Finnish sauna, and some birch tree branches. Picture meeting a very successful Italian financier who resembled Robert DeNiro, and said about as much, who was also completely naked, seated about two feet from me. All I could think about was that he knew I was sleeping with his daughter. As my presumed punishment, he kept pouring water on the hot rocks. I could feel it hit me like a punch in the chest and each time he announced the rising temperature. Then he asked, no told me, to hit myself with a tree branch to stimulate the blood flow. In between strikes, I tried to make small talk but all I could muster to say was, "So you like Formula 1?" His answer was, "Yes, Adam, I do." Fuck me. After about twenty minutes (which felt like two hours) I put my bathrobe on and walked out to find my future (now ex) wife and (now former) mother-in-law snickering. It turned out Mr. DeNiro never went in the sauna before or after our interview. I guess I passed.

The only advice my ex-father in law ever gave me as I embarked on my finance career was, "Make sure you wear a white dress shirt." I thought I'd pass on that sage advice. Yes that's sarcasm speaking and yes that's also the longest sentence I ever heard him say.

3) Should I just move to New York City (or London) without a job in hand?

> I certainly wish I had but fear of the unknown (and being unemployed in one of the world's most expensive city) got the better of me. It comes down to probability, and the probability is greater landing an i-banking job being in the city where the jobs are located. From a networking perspective, it's a lot easier (and economical) to catch the train to meet someone in town. The money you will spend landing the job will be paid back countless times over (that's what we call a great ROI). If you find yourself in a city or town and wonder why you aren't getting any i-banking jobs, perhaps you need to go to where the jobs are.

4) What's it like to be a woman in finance?

> I get this question a lot and it always amazes me. It's not that I think women don't belong in finance; they do. It amazes me because I am not a woman so I can't really answer the question. If you want to know what it's like to be a woman in finance, please ask a woman in finance. What a great topic for networking, but please don't ask it if you are a guy.

5) Should I take the sure thing in back office or hold out for the front office?

It's a tough decision but also a good problem to have. Do you go for the brand name bank and tell everyone you work for Goldman, but leave off the operations piece? Do you say no to Goldman operations and hold out for the M&A gig? It's a hard one. If you take the ops job thinking you will transition to the front office in short order, you're probably wrong and your "brown suit" colleagues will dislike you for it. On the other hand, it can be done; I've seen it first-hand and have helped people make the transition. Ultimately it has to be part of your story. Saying no to Goldman without anything else in hand can also be challenging. What if you never get the offer you wanted? Would you have been better off taking a job you didn't really want to have the brand cache? I'd ask yourself the question, before taking or decline the ops job, would you be happy doing that the rest of your life realizing you may never work in the front office? If the answer is yes, then take it. If the answer is no, then you should walk.

6) Is the lifestyle as hard as they say it is?

Yes, but it comes in waves, which makes it bearable. The stories you hear are not to scare you (well maybe a little); they are real. You will work your butt off. Your relationships will suffer as you blow off friends (and sadly even family) for work. People will think you've changed, and you probably will. You will be constantly tired, stressed and maybe even a little angry. I'd like to say it gets better the more senior you get, but I've yet to meet a happy MD.

Can you take a vacation as an investment banker? Yes, absolutely you can, but the timing of those vacations can be a bit challenging. I decided in my third year of banking to take a two-week trip to Africa to go on safari (after not taking a vacation during the first two years out of pure fear, and having promised my then wife that the third year wouldn't be more of the same). I told (asked?) my MDs about nine months out and the response I got was, "That's awesome. I've always wanted to do that." About six months out, I started working on a deal I believed would wrap up by vacation time so

I again told my MDs to which they replied, "It's going to be an amazing trip, Adam." About three months out the deal was on track and I was starting to accumulate things for the trip. I told my MDs once more. "Great, please take lots of pictures, I can't wait to see them." Well, about a month out from my trip the deal starts to go a bit sideways and I walk into my MD's (Roger) office and again remind him that I'll be going on vacation soon and his response was, "Well, you do what you think is right." What the fuck? I went to James, like a kid goes to his other parent when the first response was unsatisfactory, and he said, "Will they have internet there?" At this point, I was thinking, "Fuck me. I hate this job." Well, rather than face the wrath of a more irate than usual wife, I decided to go.

Two weeks passed and when I returned the deal was still stalled. I closed it a few weeks later. Of note, one night I was at a bar and spotted a guy wearing Gucci loafers and pressed pants. Right away I thought, "There is a Goldman Sachs banker." I thought his attire a bit strange being that we were on a fairly remote island in Malawi, but I struck up a conversation. He was traveling with his three boys who looked like they would rather be anywhere else and they had just come from their ranch in another African country. He pulled out a picture of his rhinoceros. He had a few. Sure enough, he was a managing director from one of Goldman's European offices. I never asked for his card; what a missed networking opportunity.

7) How difficult is it to transition from consulting to investment banking?

It can be done. The more time you spend doing something else however, the more challenging it is to transfer to i-banking. Each day your story evolves and if it's evolving away from finance then it's harder to create a finance story.

The skills involved in consulting are very similar to i-banking. At the end of the day professional services is all about serving a customer's needs. In i-banking, your job is largely focused around some sort of transaction, like obtaining financing or performing an acquisition. In consulting, the need revolves around solving a problem the company is facing, like sales have decreased. There is overlap in doing financial related consulting. In fact, there is a whole field known as "transaction advisory services" that applies consulting to the world of M&A. The consultants get paid to do things like find targets to acquire, project potential merger synergies and determine how much the client should pay. The consultants normally hand the deal off to the bankers and lawyers to consummate the transaction, but as soon as the ink dries, the consultants are there to help realize those synergies in a post merger integration engagement. The bankers and lawyers don't stick around unless another transaction is needed.

As for anyone transitioning from something other than finance to i-banking, you need to make it a part of your story. For example, if you used to work in information technology, you might craft your story towards technology investment banking. If you worked in healthcare, you might want to craft your story to healthcare investment banking. This is the quickest way in and it's all about your story.

8) Do I need an MBA or CFA to be an i-banker?

> No. In fact, I recommend you work as soon as you can at an investment bank. The first two years on the job will be a first class MBA. Should you need a break after a few years, school will always be there and perhaps even paid for by your employer. The CFA speaks volumes about your commitment to finance. You don't need a CFA to be an i-banker. The CFA is usually reserved for those on the asset management or equity investing side of the house. All things equal, any financial related accolade on your resume will help your story and differentiate you from others. Do them when you are young(ish) because your life will only get more busy.

9) I took some time to serve in the military and now after going back to school, I'd like to apply my skills to the i-banking world but I'm a little older than most. Should I even try?

> Yes. Absolutely. The finance world hires a lot of former military, largely for their work ethic and

leadership (which includes being able to follow) abilities. As for the age question, you get a pass as you can account for the "time away" in your story.

Do I ever think someone can be too old to work in i-banking? Yes. Not to discriminate but let's be real. If you don't get an analyst role by your mid to late twenties or an associate role by your late twenties to very early thirties, I'd think about another career. That said, the lower ends of those ranges are for the bulge bracket banks and the higher ends for the middle market to boutique banks. Look, I'm not saying don't try, but why subject yourself to that kind of lifestyle (and perhaps pay cut) after you've become accustomed to another lifestyle. From the bank's angle, the more habits you form outside of banking, the less they feel they will be able to mold you like they want.

10) What do most people do after i-banking?

I always tell people that you can do whatever you want after i-banking and I truly mean that. The skills you learn will prepare you for many different career paths ranging from corporate finance to consulting to working at a start-up to creating your own company. It's very normal for a client to hire a banker away to work on their corporate development (internal M&A and strategy) or finance team. We call this "going native" and it's the usual ticket out.

11) I'm not from the US and am worried about the bank sponsoring me. Should I even try?

> Yes you should try. Banks are set up to work with internationals. While I appreciate the odds may feel more stacked against you, don't let that stop you.

12) I have more than one offer, what should I do?

> First, be thankful, it is a good problem to have. It is also common. I say you need to weigh the pros and cons of each, realizing you don't have perfect information. Make a choice and realize you likely won't be in any one job forever. As for those who have already accepted an offer but want to accept another, that's a hard choice to make, and one I

know many face. You need to weigh what is best for you with potentially alienating a company from future employment. To put it in perspective, it's a much more important decision for you. The company will get over it.

13) What is the typical day like in i-banking?

Please don't ever ask in an interview, "What is the typical day in the life of a banker?" There is not a typical day. Each day is different. That's what keeps it interesting but also what makes it challenging.

A banker's life can best be described as interruption driven. As such you will need to get good at multi-tasking and being able to give multiple things your full attention. A typical day may look like:

- 9:30am – show up to office and answer emails; the reason you're rolling in a bit late is because you were up late the night before; you'll also have been checking your email since the time you woke up
- 10am – meeting with associate to review a pitch book you've been working on the past few days;

- last night he gave you some changes to make and this morning will be a review of those edits
- 10:30am – meeting with another associate and VP prior to a call with the client to review a first draft of an information memorandum; you scramble to make some last minute changes prior to the call
- 11:00am – conference call with associate, VP and client to review memorandum; about an hour of changes were noted which you've been tasked to make
- 12:00pm – run outside to grab some food
- 12:30pm – back at desk eating while catching up on email; you've just been selected for another deal team and your kick off meeting will be at 6pm tonight
- 1:00pm – start making some of the edits to the pitch book but phone rings and an associate wants to talk about kick-off meeting tonight; you've been asked to pull some materials together in preparation for the meeting
- 2:00pm – back to making edits to the pitch book when colleague stops by to ask if you want to grab a coffee; you ask a few others and run out with the order

- 2:30pm – back at desk and continue to make edits to pitch book when you get an email forwarded from associate looking for comps from a deal you just worked on
- 3:00pm – get an email from associate asking if pitch book is done yet; you need another hour or two
- 4:00pm – finished pulling together materials for kick-off meeting at 6pm and send to associate for review
- 5:00pm – finish making edits to the pitch book and send it to the associate for review
- 5:30pm – receive edits from associate and make changes to kick off materials
- 6:00pm – kick off meeting; you are asked to pull together a public information book (PIB) for the deal by tomorrow as well as pull an initial comp set
- 7:00pm – you go around the office collecting everyone's dinner order and put it into the online ordering system; in the meantime you decide to go out for a short run
- 8:00pm – you eat dinner around the conference table with a few of the analysts and associates; the senior bankers start to leave

- 9:00pm – done with dinner you go back to your desk and answer some emails; the senior folks at the bank have all left so the VPs and associates start to leave; you can now get some work done
- 10:00pm – you make additional changes to the pitch book that your associate sent
- 12:00am – you make changes to the information memorandum and send back to your internal team for review
- 2:00am – you're done creating the PIB for the new deal you're working on; you're aiming to come in a little early tomorrow morning to get an early start on the comps
- 2:30am – answer last emails for the night; call an Uber and go home

14) Right but what do I really do?

The process of doing a deal is not second nature for companies. While it is true that some companies do more deals than others, it is still not in a company's DNA to buy another company or do a financing.

You should think of your role as moving the ball forward a little each day. Use the football field analogy. You start at one goal line and move a little each day towards the other goal line. All along the way there are obstacles in your way. Without you driving the ball forward, the deal would die.

As for what an M&A process looks like, there are four primary phases. Let's review each phase (for a deal where you are taking a client to market in a sell-side deal) and your role:

1. Preparation
    a. Formulate strategy for taking company to market and create buyer list
    b. Set a timeline for the deal and manage customer expectations for how long it might take and their required commitment
    c. Create marketing materials like a one pager, information memorandum, etc.
    d. Create initial valuation materials
2. Reach Out & Preliminary Assessment
    a. Create, send and negotiate NDAs with prospective buyers

b. Send marketing materials once NDAs executed
   c. Allow buyers to do cursory due diligence
   d. Assess potential buyer interest and filter to a few parties that want to move forward
3. Meeting & Negotiations
   a. Schedule meetings for parties to meet
   b. Ask buyers for letters of intent (non-binding) to see if they are interested and in the ballpark of valuation
   c. Continue due diligence process
4. Closing
   a. Draft final documentation & terms of deal
   b. Negotiate and sign Definitive Agreement (binding)
   c. Do SEC filings
   d. Close deal

You can think of a junior banker's role as being the glue that holds the deal together. Your activity is greater at the start and end of a deal. Think of your role as primarily: 1) creating and managing all marketing documents, 2) creating and managing all valuation materials, 3) documenting who said what when, and 4) creating status reports on the deal. Those higher in the pecking order are there to make sure you do your job right and that all parties are doing what they should as the process roles along. Those even higher up are managing the personal relationships and negotiations and making sure the deal stays on track.

As for the time commitment in a deal, you might consider a U shaped graph where phase 1 and phase 4 require the most work. Using the same football analogy, think of it as getting out of your own end zone and then scoring a touchdown on the other end. Not to say charging down the middle of the field isn't hard, but going from stop to start and culminating the deal are hard and require more effort.

15) What are the different finance jobs I should be thinking about?

There are many different types of finance jobs. Your job is to understand the differences and apply them as you develop your story. Let's think about it in broad strokes. First, there are those who have the money and are looking to put it to work, primarily to make more money. Then there are those who need the money, and also looking to put it to work, for various reasons. Then there are those who are helping both sides to achieve their goals primarily by working with equity and debt investment vehicles.

As for those who have the money, it can range from hedge funds and asset managers to university endowments and high net worth individuals (with the last two often relying on the first two to invest their money). These entities are often referred to as the "buy side". The reason is that they buy investments with the goal of making more money. Private equity, or firms that buy other companies, is a great example of putting money to work to make a high return.

Investment banks serve the "buy side". This includes working on their behalf to find them an investment. For example, if a PE shop hires a bank to acquire a public company, often known as a leveraged buyout (LBO), that would be known as a "buy side" deal.

A bank can also act as the "sell-side" to those with the money. When a bank sells advice or offers of a security, debt or equity, they are referred to as the "sell side". The bank and its investment bankers make money when a client buys something, specifically the security they are selling. Another job included in this capacity is equity research. An equity research analyst covers a particular asset class or type of company and puts out recommendations for the buy side to hopefully make more money. For example, there are about 25 individuals worldwide who do nothing but live, breathe and sleep Apple. Their job is to put out recommendations on whether or not to buy Apple's stock.

Banks also execute the sale and trading of particular securities. The "front office" is selling the security and often "making a market" while the "back office" manages the operations surrounding the buying and selling of securities. This includes everything from keeping records to maintaining regulatory oversight.

As for those who need the money, it can range from corporations to municipalities. For example, a corporation may need money to acquire a company or build a new factory. A municipality may need capital to build a new bridge. In all cases, they are hoping to use money (at a specific cost) and put it to work to make more than the cost. Finance professionals work for these companies and municipalities as well. Think corporate finance, financial planning & analysis, treasury, and corporate development.

Investment banks help those entities raise money as well as put it to work. This is known as capital markets. The banker will work hand in hand with the company's finance team to determine the type of security (debt or equity) and the underlying value of the company. For example, when Facebook went public, there were a few banks (a syndicate) who had the job of determining their underlying valuation and therefore what price to offer the securities at IPO. The banker will then help sell those securities (the bank actually buys and resells them to the public market). The same hold true with debt, through bonds. After the company has money to put to work, it may want to buy a company. For example, after Facebook went public, it had enough cash to buy What's App, and it likely employed a bank to negotiate the deal.

As you think about the person who is interviewing you, think about a few things:
1) do they have the money, need the money, or which side are they helping (buy side or sell side),
2) what is being bought or sold, namely debt or equity
3) in what vertical(s) are they operating (i.e. transportation, manufacturing, technology, municipalities, etc.)
4) what is the end goal of the transaction, (i.e. merger, financing a project, etc.)

If you understand the above, you'll know whom you're talking to in the interview.

16) Should I just apply to any and all finance jobs?

The answer is absolutely and unequivocally no. The shotgun approach does not work. In fact, what the bank sees if you apply to every open position, is you don't know what you want to do so you shouldn't get any job. I know that sounds unfair and it is, but look at it from their angle. You don't have a story.

In business school, I and many of my classmates, always had much more success when applying for only one job (M&A) at a bank versus multiple jobs (Operations, Sales & Trading and M&A). It bucks everything you think about with regard to probability, but probability is not relevant here.

Shortly out of b-school, a very good friend of mine, who was a consultant, got two offers from different groups at Goldman Sachs at the same time. When HR found out and communicated to both hiring managers, they pulled both offers. Neither wanted someone that didn't have their story straight.

17) What are the main differences between boutique and bulge bracket banks?

>Everyone wants to work for Goldman Sachs and why not? It is associated with prestige and wealth. They do the deals everyone wants to work on. Odds are the merger you are reading about on the front cover of the Wall St. Journal involves Goldman (or one of the other bulge banks). The problem is that Goldman only hires a few hundred analysts and associates each year. The bulge brackets have thousands of people and it would be great to be another among the ranks. Think about how your story applies to a bulge bracket bank.

>The next tier down is the middle-market bank. You can think of these as largely geographically focused, for example they cover the southeast United States. It is possible that they can actually do more deals a year than the bulge brackets. That's volume not dollars. They are staffed with hundreds of people. To be one of those hundred, think about how geography and size might apply to your story.

The next tier down is the boutique bank. These banks can be located anywhere and everywhere. They are largely focused on particular verticals. The banks may have anywhere from 5 to 50 people. Often the MDs have spun out from the bulge or middle-markets and are happy working for themselves. On average, they do only a few deals a year, maybe ten at most. There are more boutique-sized deals than middle market or bulge. Why? Well because there are many more small companies. To be one of the boutique's next hires, how does their focus area and smaller team match your story?

The hiring process differs greatly across the various types of banks. The bulge brackets run a formal hiring process which is well managed and you will need to play their game to get a job there. They usually hire the same number (+/- a few depending on the economy) each year, so absolutely give it a go, but realize that the numbers are working against you. The middle-market banks also run a fairly formal hiring process but it may be a little off cycle with the bulge brackets. It could also be more geographically focused than the bulge banks. They are largely whipsawed by the economy and may be behind in their hiring needs. The boutique banks will likely run a haphazard process at best. They may hire you because they are beyond busy or, if they like you, they could hire you to add to their bench strength even if they are not at full capacity. The boutiques are a bit of a crapshoot, but there's opportunity to be had in rolling those dice.

18) Can I make money at a smaller bank?

Yes. Let's visit the economics of banking. If you're at a bulge bracket which does a $10B deal and makes a 5% fee, that's $500M to the bank. After taxes that's $250M. Now take another half for that nice office building downtown, and you're left with $125M. Take another 50% for the other groups in the bank who didn't fare as well and you're left with $63M. Now, share a little of that with the partners and let's assume you're left with $35M to split across a ten to twenty person deal team, with those on top making more than those on the bottom. Not a bad year any way you cut it.

If you're at a boutique bank, which did a $100M deal and made a 5% fee then that's $5M to the bank. After Uncle Sam, you make $2.5M. No need to fund the expensive office or the other teams. The deal team will also be much smaller with maybe two to five people, perhaps a little less shaped like a pyramid. Assume you do a few of those a year and I'm sure you wouldn't turn it down either.

Made in the USA
Columbia, SC
20 September 2019